Marriage
BY
THE
BOOK

Biblical Models for Marriage Today

BOB RUSSELL

STANDARD
PUBLISHING
Cincinnati, Ohio

This book is dedicated to my father and my mother:

Charles and Catherine Russell

Their example of a godly marriage has been an inspiration to me and many others for more than fifty years.

A special thanks also goes to my wife Judy, who has helped me experience the love, joy, fulfillment, and security of marriage as God intended it to be.

Unless otherwise noted, all Scriptures are quoted from *The Holy Bible: New International Version*, ©1973, 1978, 1984 by the International Bible Society. Used by permission of Zondervan Bible Publishers.

Library of Congress Cataloging-in-Publication Data:

Russell, Bob, 1943-
   Marriage by the book : biblical models for marriage today / Bob Russell.
     p. cm.
   ISBN 0-87403-906-1
   1. Marriage—Biblical teaching. 2. Bible. O.T.—Criticism, interpretation, etc. I. Title.
BS1199.M3R87   1992
248.8'44—dc20   91-917
                                             CIP

CONTENTS

FOREWORD

by Steve and Annie Chapman

We don't know how many times we have purchased some type of technical or electronic gadget and have made the same mistake. We get it home, tear into the box, take out the new item, and immediately attempt to use it. Within moments we are scratching our heads, wondering why in the world it's not performing its designated function.

Eventually, we come to our senses and we remember what the problem is. Again, we've ignored that step in the process that is most important. As we tore into the box, somehow we assumed that that plastic bag with the owner's manual was really just packing. Surely, it's not that important. That's where we went wrong.

There is something in which many of us have invested that can be far more complex than any technical item available to the human—it's called marriage. How many of us have come home, opened the wedding package, and immediately tried to operate with intelligence only to discover in a little while that we're totally puzzled. Some are more than perplexed at how marriage should work; they begin to wonder why they even invested in it in the first place.

The obvious point is this: there is an owner's manual that comes with marriage. The Word of God contains that information.

Many times, as we opened the owner's manual that accompanied those gadgets we mentioned, we discovered that there were parts of that manual that were not easily understood. So, it is true with the Lord's instructions on marriage found in the Scriptures. We often need help in understanding the manual.

Let us introduce you now to Bob Russell's *Marriage by the Book.* You have in your hands some valuable insights about the real "manual" God wants us to understand—which is His Word. *Marriage by the Book* will be one of the most helpful tools you'll possess in your marriage. Whether you're a marriage veteran, newlywed, or engaged, the pages to follow will be useful on a daily basis.

We have been inspired by many aspects of Bob Russell's ministry, including his sermons and his fellowship. (We've even used some of his ideas in our songs.) However, the one thing that inspires us most is his own devotion to Judy. It is from his own experience in understanding the "manual" that this information is offered. As you consume these pages, be assured that you will be assisted in one of the greatest of desires God has for couples and that is a "Marriage by the Book."

INTRODUCTION

The more I study God's Word, the more impressed I am with the practical wisdom it provides in every area. That is the reason I believe there is great value in studying Old Testament characters and events. Paul wrote, "These things happened to them as examples and were written down for us, on whom the fulfillment of the ages has come" (1 Corinthians 10:11). There is something enlightening to me about studying how God dealt with His people under the Old Covenant. There is much to learn from their successes and failures.

Marriage in the Old Testament days was far from ideal. However, we can still learn from the experiences of the patriarchs about what God intends marriage in the Christian era to be. An analysis of the home life of some Old Testament heroes will serve as the basis for this study.

I believe the Bible reveals better than any other source the secret of a harmonious marriage. It beats every marriage manual, every enrichment seminar, and every trained counselor. There is certainly value in books, seminars, and counselors, but God's Word is a distinctive "lamp unto our feet and light unto our path" (Psalm 119:105).

It is my prayer that the following chapters will assist you in establishing a marriage by *The Book*—the Bible—which is the "living and enduring word of God" (1 Peter 1:23).

1

FOCUS ON THE IDEAL

(ADAM AND EVE)

Scene magazine carried a feature article in the March 9, 1991, issue entitled "Alone Together." It related that America now has more than two and a half million unmarried couples living together. That's a million more than in 1980. It said the increase in the number of cohabiting couples is another sign that the typical American family isn't what it used to be.

The increase in live-in relationships is also a sign that people are very disillusioned today with marriage. In the article, one man explained his live-in relationship this way: "I always said I would never marry someone until I lived with them. I know too many people who have gotten married without living together and found out it was a mistake." Another couple has a merged family: each one has two children from a previous marriage, and they now have a child of their own. But, since they are not married, they don't know what last name to give to their month-old daughter. "There is no question that we are committed to each other," the woman said, "but each of us has been married and divorced twice, and we see no need to get married again."

I strongly disagree with the concept of living together without marriage. The Bible calls it fornication and warns us to flee from it because of the dire consequences that it has. But I can understand how some people can be disillusioned with marriage. Many of them have been deeply wounded by marital relationships, or they have seen friends in unsuccessful marriages, and they don't want that to happen to them.

One guy says, "Marriage is kind of like a hot bath. Once you become accustomed to it, it's not so hot." But somehow people are convinced that the problem is in the marriage relationship itself, or in the institution of marriage, rather than in the expectations and the behavior of the people involved.

But as thousands of people will testify, a live-in relationship ultimately produces more complications and heartaches. It's interesting that the article in *Scene* was entitled *"Alone* Together." There is something about living together without the commitment of marriage that produces insecurity and ultimately loneliness.

The solution is not abandoning the institution of marriage, but returning to God's intention of what marriage was supposed to be. Satan is attacking the family with a vengeance. It is imperative, then, that we frequently go back and reinforce our foundations. One way to do that is to look at several marriages in the Bible. These can teach us some helpful lessons about what God intended the home to be.

Let's begin by looking at Adam and Eve, the first marriage. A river is purest at its source, and the first union should represent for us the ideal. By studying Adam and Eve, we should be able to elevate our appreciation of what marriage is designed to be.

Purpose

Notice first of all that the first marriage was a purposeful marriage. A look at Genesis 2:18 reveals that God established marriage for the purpose of companionship. "The Lord God said, 'It is not good for the man to be alone. I will make a helper suitable for him.'" The word *helper* means ally or friend. God knew His creation exactly. He knew that man does not usually function well alone. Statistics show that single men generally do not live as long as married men. And a widower doesn't live as long as married men his age unless he remarries.

A survey was taken some time ago of four categories of people: married and unmarried men, married and unmarried women. The intent was to see which category of people were the happiest. At the top, the happiest people, were most often married men. The unhappiest were unmarried men, because it's not good for man to be alone.

(Strangely, the second happiest people were unmarried women. I don't understand that, but that is what the report said.)

God knew that man does not function well alone, that he needed a companion, so God took action. Verse 19: "The Lord God had formed out of the ground all the beasts of the field and all the birds of the air. He brought them to the man to see what he would name them; and whatever the man called each living creature, that was its name." Isn't that a strange sequence of Scripture? God said it's not good that man be alone, and the next thing He did was to parade these animals by man. Apparently, God was demonstrating to Adam the need for companionship. While Adam enjoyed the animals, they certainly couldn't supply his need for partnership or communication. After looking at hippopotamuses and monkeys and giraffes and lizards, a woman was going to look very good to Adam!

So Adam named all the livestock, and then God did something incredible: He performed the first surgery. Look at verse 21. "So the Lord God caused the man to fall into deep sleep"; there's the first anesthesia. "And while he was sleeping, he took one of man's ribs and closed up the place with flesh. Then the Lord God made a woman from the rib he had taken out of the man, and he brought her to the man."

Of course, God could have formed woman from the dust of the ground the same way that He had formed man. He chose instead to begin with the rib from Adam's side to show the unique closeness of this relationship that He had designed. The old rabbi said, "God chose a rib from Adam's side, not a bone from Adam's head that she would be over him, or a bone from his foot that she would be under him, but from his side that she would be next to him, from under his arm that he might protect her, and from next to his heart that he might love her." This was symbolic of the closeness of the companionship God intended between a husband and a wife.

When Adam awakened after this deep sleep, he saw standing before him this gorgeous creature, the first woman he had ever

seen. She was almost like him, but she was wonderfully different. And—verse 23—"The man said, 'This is now bone of my
bones and flesh of my flesh.'" Now, you know that has to lose
something in translation. *The Living Bible* paraphrases it, "'This
is it!' Adam exclaimed. 'She is part of my own bone and flesh.'"
So Adam and Eve formed this companionship: sexually, emotionally, and spiritually.

Marriage is not the only way people have close companionship
with others. Some single people have closer companionship with
people than some married people have. But a marriage relationship has the highest potential for companionship because it is
designed for companionship.

Genesis 1:28 reveals another purpose for marriage. God established marriage for the purpose of rearing children. "God blessed
them and said to them, 'Be fruitful and increase in number; fill
the earth and subdue it.'" God gave us sexual desires so that we
have a wonderful way to express our love to our mates, and He
created us with those desires so that we would replenish the
earth. But God specified that sex was to be enjoyed in the parameters of marriage so that the children would grow up with a
source of security and a moral environment. It was never God's
intention that there would be unwanted babies who would be
discarded. It was never God's intention that children would have
low self-esteem and they would roam the streets unsupervised
because the parents didn't care.

The television program *48 Hours* did a brief documentary on
"Spring Break" a while back. Among the many seventeen- and
eighteen-year-old girls that were featured, several were from
Louisville. They were guzzling beer and finalizing plans to spend
the night with some young men in a motel room.

On the local (Louisville) news that followed, these girls were
interviewed. The girls boasted and laughed about their activity
and bragged about what a good time they had had. What I found
most incredible was an interview with the mother of one of the
girls. She was asked how she felt about her daughter's indulging
in that kind of activity on "Spring Break," and the mother casually said, "Oh, I don't see that she did anything wrong. She had a

good time, and that is what 'Spring Break' is all about, having a good time."

How could a mother be aware of the deadly consequences of alcohol and of A.I.D.S. and not be concerned about such behavior? God never intended for children to grow up without moral standards. He established the relationship of marriage so that people would love each other and love their children enough to give them protective moral values. That is one of the purposes of marriage, and it is a missing ingredient in many homes today.

There is yet another purpose of marriage. It is not just for companionship and for child rearing. Genesis 2:24 demonstrates that marriage is for a testimony. This verse of Scripture is repeated four times in the Bible for emphasis. "For this reason a man will leave his father and mother and be united to his wife, and they will become one flesh."

For what reason are people to get married? Oh, we always say they are supposed to get married for love. But the Bible doesn't say that. In fact, Adam and Eve were married apparently the first day. They grew to love each other, but they didn't get married because they loved each other. There is a mysterious reason suggested here, a mystery that isn't cleared up until the final time this verse of Scripture is used. It's in the book of Ephesians, the fifth chapter, verses 31 and 32:

> "For this reason a man will leave his father and mother and be united to his wife, and the two will become one flesh." This is a profound mystery—but I am talking about Christ and the church.

A Christian marriage is to be a positive testimony to the world of Christ's love for the church. God's love is unconditional. It is faithful. It is sacrificial. So when there is a Christian marriage that is unconditional, faithful, and sacrificial, it's a testimony to the world of how God loves man. And when a Christian marriage breaks up, there is a double tragedy. Not only does it affect the immediate family, but the world says, "Ah, there's no difference; God's love doesn't make any difference."

Two of the three purposes for marriage are unselfish. Marriage does supply our need for companionship, but it has a deeper purpose: it meets the need for a stable environment for children and for a positive testimony to the world. In fact, when the marriage is ideal, one desires to provide companionship for the other person more than himself, and the whole marriage is unselfish. When a person lives together with somebody without marriage, it is almost always a selfish decision: I am protecting me. God calls us to a nobler cause than that. He calls us to a life of unselfishness and obedience and a testimony to the world.

Exclusive

There is a second factor that made Adam and Eve's relationship ideal: it was an exclusive relationship. When that first couple got married, they had no one else in mind. Adam was the only man; Eve was the only woman. Adam wasn't standing at the altar wondering whether there might be somebody better. Eve didn't look back years later and say, "I wonder what would have happened if I had married the captain of the football team." There was no option. There was no competition, no comparison, no other offer.

(I did hear that Eve became concerned one night because Adam didn't come in until 3:00 A.M. and she wondered if there was another woman. So she waited until he was asleep and counted his ribs just to make sure!)

But Eve was the only one available, so Adam didn't compare her to somebody else and feel deprived. Eve didn't complain that Adam wasn't as romantic as somebody that she had seen on television. There was no insecurity in their relationship. They were committed to each other exclusively.

Unlike that first couple, we are surrounded by hundreds of comparisons and choices every day. A lot of married people are continually looking over their shoulders, wondering whether they made the right choice, wondering whether there is somebody else who would make them happier. But a Christian marriage is not based on the premise that I've won the top prize available. It's based on the premise that this is the person God has provided for me and I'm going to be the best companion I can be—to this one exclusively. That eliminates insecurity, and it provides the way for real companionship and love.

Years ago, when I was younger, I used to get a lot of offers from other churches to come be their preacher. Southeast was smaller then, but it was growing rapidly, so larger churches that could pay a larger salary would contact me and ask me to consider being their preacher. I would listen to them, and it would make me a little restless, and I would compare. Sometimes I'd talk with the pulpit committee or with the elders, and then I would feel obligated to them, and I would go through a real period of churning to make a decision. Then one day I made a different decision: I decided I was not going to entertain any other offers. I was going to stay at Southeast. That made things so much easier: it eliminated that period of restlessness, it made me happier. I quit making comparisons. I seldom get an offer to move anymore. I guess it's because the word is out I'm not movable—at least, I hope that is the reason. But if I began to make it known that I was looking to go someplace else, I'm sure some offers would come again.

The same is true in your marriage. If you want the most fulfilling relationship, there needs to be a mental exclusiveness about your marriage. One author said you need to "murder the alternatives," and if you didn't mean it when you said to your partner at the altar, "I'm going to give myself to you only till death do us part," then you need to begin to mean it now. As long as you're comparing, you are going to be disgruntled and restless; you will pick at your partner and wonder whether you could do better. But if you really want God's best, murder the alternatives. And there is a sense in which that has to be repeated every day because you send out signals all the time about whether you are willing to relocate.

One attractive woman executive said she deliberately takes steps to offset any overtures at the office. She has a picture of her husband and family in a very prominent place, and when she is involved in conversation with another man she quickly works in some reference to her husband, very early in the conversation, and she talks about some of the fun things that they have done together as a family. I guarantee you, that immediate signal has closed doors early and contributed to the lasting happy relationship in that home. Jesus said it like this, "'For this reason a man will leave his father and mother and be united to his wife, and the two will become one flesh.' . . . Therefore what God has joined together, let man not separate" (Matthew 19:5, 6).

Transparent

Adam and Eve's relationship was also ideal because it was a transparent relationship. Genesis 2:25 is a significant verse: "The man and his wife were both naked, and they felt no shame." Since there was no sin, there was nothing to hide. No deception, no inhibitions—everything was perfect. He was never late or preoccupied with his work. Eve never burned anything or spent too much money with a credit card. There were no bills, no physical defects, no clothing to buy. No in-laws. Everything was perfect for a romantic relationship.

Then sin entered the garden, and everything was spoiled. You know the story: Satan persuaded Eve to eat of the forbidden fruit, and she immediately persuaded Adam to eat. Genesis 3:7 reads like this: "Then the eyes of both of them were opened, and they realized they were naked; so they sewed fig leaves together and made coverings for themselves." Sin made them self-conscious. It gave them inhibitions in marriage. Sin alienated them from God and from each other.

J. Grant Howard has written a book called *The Trauma of Transparency* in which he points out that Adam and Eve present the classic case of two results of sin.[1] Number one: when we sin, we hide from God and from each other. Number two: when we are pressed, we hurl accusations against God and each other. When God asked Adam, "Why did you sin?" he said, "Well, that woman You gave me, she made me eat." And when God said to Eve, "Why did you eat?" she said, "Well, the serpent made me

[1]J. Grant Howard, *The Trauma of Transparency* (Portland: Multnomah, 1979).

eat." And ever since, man's been blaming his wife and the wife's been calling her husband a snake, and there have been problems. Howard says, "Before, they were perfectly contented with how they looked, but now they wear masks."

Please note: as one's relationship matures spiritually, it should produce an increasing transparency with his mate. Now, we will never achieve the total transparency that Adam and Eve knew in the Garden of Eden. Be careful not to take this concept of openness too far. Everybody needs some space. Everybody needs some privacy, including your mate. There is a sense in which you will never know everything about your partner. You don't even know everything about yourself. But the closer we get to the ideal, the more honest, transparent, and uninhibited we can be with each other. You can't be close to somebody from whom you're keeping a lot of secrets. There is not much room in a marriage for intentional deception. God's ideal was for total transparency in marriage. That is a part of the uniqueness of the relationship. That begins with an open, honest sharing of your thoughts when you are dating, and it includes sexual intimacy in marriage without inhibitions.

One study related that sixty percent of married couples are frustrated in their sexual relationship. Sixty percent!

Redbook magazine, however, did a national survey, and they came up with a conclusion that really surprised them. They wrote, "The greater the intensity of a woman's spiritual commitment, the more likely her satisfaction with sexual pleasure in marriage." You see, when Adam and Eve were in their perfect state, they were uninhibited with each other, and the closer we get to the Lord the fewer inhibitions there should be in a marriage. If you have a lot of sexual hang-ups in your marriage relationship, you did not get that from the Lord; you got that from the adversary. You need to reprogram your mind through Scripture. Read the Song of Solomon, a beautiful celebration of love between Solomon and his beloved.

But transparency has to do with more than sexual relationships. It has to do with the sharing of inner thoughts and feelings. One group of counselors estimated that eighty-five percent of all marriage problems come down to poor communication. One article said that the average couple spends forty-seven hours a week watching television and only thirty minutes a week talking and listening to each other. Proverbs 13:17 in *The Living Bible* reads, "Reliable communication permits progress." The more honest and open and reliable your communication, the more your marriage is going to grow. That means we have to say what we are thinking, and it means we have to pay attention and listen. My wife tells me that I don't listen to her sometimes. (At least, I think that's what she said.) It's not easy. Honesty is risky, because we fear rejection. So many couples go through their marriage pretending that all is well when in reality the communication is so shallow that there is little companionship and there is a lot of loneliness.

Scott Peck, in one of his books,[2] talks about "authentic relationships" and "pseudo relationships." Authentic relationships are those relationships where we are completely honest with each other and we can deepen in our understanding. But pseudo relationships are those relationships where we pretend all is well, but there are a number of subjects that we just don't touch on. We don't talk about the husband's work ethic, or we don't talk about the wife's weight, because these are volatile subjects. The more subjects that you have that you're secretive about, the more "pseudo" your relationship. Couples in those relationships are pretending that everything is okay, but they are lonely.

To get from a pseudo relationship to an authentic relationship, Peck says you have to go through the "tunnel of chaos." It's a tunnel where you agree that you are both going to speak honestly and truthfully, and each one is going to listen to the other. Please note: this is not a time to be brutal. You must be loving, but you must also be open and transparent. It's a tunnel of chaos because you don't know what is going to happen in there. You can be wounded. You might come out worse than you went in, but it's essential to go into the tunnel of chaos in order to make it a

[2]M. Scott Peck, *The Different Drum* (New York: Simon & Schuster, 1987).

tunnel of love—a path to authentic relationships where you are completely honest and open with each other.

Rick Warren has a sermon entitled "The Greatest Risk You Will Ever Take." He's talking about the risk of being totally honest with your mate. It's risky, he says, because man's oldest problem is the fear of rejection. We are afraid if we really say what is on our mind, if we really open up as to what our past is like, that we are going to be rejected. We are not going to be loved and accepted. But Ephesians 4:15 reads, in *The Living Bible*, "We will lovingly follow the truth at all times—speaking truly, dealing truly, living truly—and so become more and more in every way like Christ." The more truthful we are in our marriage relationships, the more we are like Christ and the closer we get to each other.

A word of caution is in order here. To go into the tunnel of chaos, two people must voluntarily agree to do so. You can't force somebody into the tunnel of chaos. But if two people will agree to put their fears aside and take the risk of entering that tunnel, the potential reward of an improved relationship is incalculable.

I was standing with my wife in a worship service a while back, and we were singing "Great Is Thy Faithfulness." All of a sudden, she stopped singing. I looked over, and the tears were streaming down her cheeks, and she was choked up. So I just held her hand as we sang, and then, after the services as we were driving home alone, I asked her if there was something wrong. Perceptive question, wasn't it? She said, "Oh, I just got to thinking about my dad." Her father was eighty years old at the time, and she was really concerned about him. She said, "'Great is Thy Faithfulness' was my dad's favorite song, and I just remember times that I played it on the piano and he sang it. I got to thinking: you know, that is a song we ought to have sung at my dad's funeral some day." She teared up again, and I did too. But Judy's transparency with her feelings made me feel even closer to her. It made me feel a special part of her life. Her vulnerability with her feelings enhanced my love for her.

Being transparent is particularly difficult for men. It's hard for us to be transparent because one of our greatest needs is the need to be respected, and we are afraid if we let the cracks show, if we show our emotions, that our mates are going to lose respect. In reality, however, just the opposite is true. The more transparent we are, the more their love is enhanced.

One of the most common complaints of women is, "My husband won't talk to me. He used to talk all the time when we were dating. He would call me on the phone and talk. We got called down in class for talking. But now that we are married, all he does is grunt, 'uh-huh, uh-uh,' and the only time he grunts is when he wants food or sex or for me to change the channel, and I am getting a little tired of it!"

If we men want to have authentic relationships, we have to be transparent. We sometimes have to be the one to initiate the conversation. We have to be willing to pay attention. Jesus said, "You will know the truth, and the truth will set you free."

Spiritual

Finally, Adam and Eve's relationship was ideal because it was a spiritual relationship. They had perfect fellowship with God. They walked with Him in the Garden of Eden. That enhanced their relationship not only with God but with each other

Almost always when I counsel with a couple before I perform their marriage ceremony, I will draw a triangle on a piece of paper and write at the top, "God," and at the lower corners, "Husband," and "Wife." Then, tracing the ascending lines of the triangle, I will point out how the closer you get to God, the closer you will be to each other. That illustration is not original with me, but I think it demonstrates the fact that the more spiritual a marriage is, the more fulfilling it will be.

Some people are frightened when their mates begin to walk closely with God. They are afraid that a deeply spiritual life will alienate them or perhaps make their marriage boring. So the wife ascends toward God, and the husband stubbornly remains where he is—or maybe he withdraws or even goes horizontal trying to find her—but there is a distancing between the two. It's not until both husband and wife agree to grow in their spiritual relationship that they come closer to each other.

Let me list five of the marital benefits that are produced by a strong spiritual life.

Number one, *your commitment to each other is enhanced* because it's not just to another person, it's to the higher authority of God.

Number two, there is an awareness of sin that serves as a *deterrent to affairs.* If you make decisions based solely on how you feel at the moment, there is very little stability. But a Christian has an absolute standard of right and wrong that remains steady regardless of fluctuating feelings.

Number three, you have *Christian friends who enhance and reinforce your family values.* If the majority of your friends are non-Christians, then their attitude can have a domino effect on you in a negative way. But if the majority of your friends are Christians, your values are reinforced.

Number four, your *ultimate fulfillment is provided by Jesus Christ,* and you become less demanding on your mate. So many people are restless because there is a spiritual void in their lives, and they don't know what is missing. So they blame their mates for their lack of happiness. If you are looking to your mate to fulfill all of your needs, you are always going to be disappointed. You will be vulnerable to all kinds of corruption from this world. But if the Lord fulfills your spiritual needs, then you are not so demanding on your mate, and you have more of yourself left to give.

Fifth, if you grow spiritually, you learn to worship and pray together, and that acts as an *adhesive in your marriage relationship.*

A 1980 Harvard University study revealed this amazing statistic. At that time, one in three marriages was ending in divorce. But when the couple was married in a church ceremony and they attended church regularly together and they prayed and read the Bible together daily, there was only one divorce in 1,105 marriages!

When Christ is the center of the home, He brings it together. It is stupid not to put Christ at the center of your home in today's culture with the kind of pressure that we face. What a contrast between the world's philosophy of cohabitation without marriage and the Christian philosophy.

If in the dark we lose sight of love,
Hold my hand and have no fear
Because I will be here.
I will be here and you can cry on my shoulder.
When the mirror tells us that we are older,
I will hold you and watch you grow in beauty
And tell you all the things you are to me,
And I will be here.
I will be true to the promise I have made to you
And to the one who gave you to me.[3]

Adam and Eve had that kind of ideal marriage, but they did the same thing that we do: they blew it. They sinned, and all of a sudden the downward spiral began, and they were alienated from each other. But ever since that time, God has been reaching down in love to lift us up. He came in the form of Jesus Christ to die on the cross to forgive us of those mistakes we've made in the past and to bury each one. He arose from the dead to show that one day we could be resurrected and have an ideal fellowship with Him again. But in the meantime, He wants us to grow to be like Him. He wants us to reach for that ideal.

2

UNDERSTAND YOUR ROLE

(ABRAHAM AND SARAH)

A segment of our society is attempting to eliminate all distinctions between male and female. I think most of us would agree that women should have equal opportunity. It's certainly not right that a woman a few decades ago didn't even have the right to vote, and it's not right today that women don't get equal pay for equal work or have more difficulty borrowing money than men. But the issue I am speaking of is not equal opportunity, but unisexism: the intentional blurring of all distinction between genders.

You can see unisexism in little things: young men on dates don't know whether they are supposed to open the door for the young woman or not—they don't know whether they will get a word of thanks or a kick in the shin! You can see it in the bizarre, like female reporters' going into the locker room of a National Football League team, or men taking female hormones to enlarge their breasts so they can experience a bonding similar to that of of breast feeding. You can see it in more serious cases like the separation of young mothers from their nursing infants so the mothers could go off to war in the Middle East. You can see it in churches where hymns are neutralized and Scripture references to God are altered to eliminate "sexism." You can see gender blending glorified in pop culture where Madonna dresses and acts like an aggressive male, and Michael Jackson does the opposite. I understand now that one rock performer has even announced that he is both male and female.

This unisex movement assaults a basic truth of creation, that God created two distinct kinds of people, male and female. He created us with different roles—not only for the propagation of the human race—but He also did it for our own well-being. God said to Adam, "I will make a helper for you, a compliment to you. She will not be exactly like you. She will have different abilities and a different function."

Please note: men and women are equally important to God, but they are not created the same. We are not only different physically, but we are different emotionally. Studies of unborn babies have disclosed that female babies in the womb develop the left hemisphere of the brain faster than male babies. The left hemisphere is where the verbal skills originate. The right side of the male develops faster. The right side is the source of visual spatial abilities.

In another survey, a number of two- to four-year-old children were recorded at play. The study found that almost 100 percent of the girls' sounds were verbal expressions. On the other hand, nearly 40 percent of the little boys' sounds were unintelligible: "Brummm, brummm. Eek! Brummm"—you know.

Dr. James Dobson reported the average man speaks about 25,000 words a day. The average woman speaks almost 50,000 words a day. When a man comes home at the end of a day, he's got about 10 words left, and she has about 10,000 that she is ready to use!

Dr. Harold Sala points out other differences that are usually evidenced in adults. Men usually get their self-esteem from their careers; women usually through the family. Men manipulate things, while women are sensitive to people. For men, shopping is a task to be endured. For women, it's an experience to be enjoyed. Women are loyal to one television program, while men are channel changers, rushing from one to another so they don't miss anything. Men focus on facts; women, on feelings.

Now, when we deny all gender differences as chauvinistic, and young mothers go off to war and women reporters are in men's locker rooms, we are not only being unrealistic. I think we are rebelling against God's created order.

In the following pages, we are going to study what the Scripture has to say about the husband's role in marriage and the wife's role in marriage. Few of us would take a new job today without a very clear job description and an understanding of the lines of accountability. Yet, every day, people are entering into marriage, which is supposed to be the highest human relationship, without any idea of what roles they are supposed to play.

If you have not submitted to the lordship of Jesus Christ, and if the Bible is not the authority in your life, then you are going to have a real problem with some of what I have to say in this chapter. If you have bought into the wisdom of this age, then you will instinctively resist this teaching. But the Bible says, as Christians, we are not to be conformed to this world; we are to be transformed by the renewing of our minds (Romans 12:1, 2). The Christian has to think counter-culture. So, before you dismiss everything that I say as chauvinistic or old-fashioned, would you please remember a statistic from the previous chapter? One in three marriages today ends in divorce, but in a marriage where the couple is married in the church building and they attend church regularly together, and they read the Bible and pray together daily, it's one divorce in 1,105 marriages. So if it works, isn't it worth your objective evaluation?

The Husband's Role

Our model for this study will be Abraham and Sarah. They are one of the first couples about whom much is written after Adam and Eve. Let's look first at the role of Abraham, which was that of a *Christlike leader*. Genesis 12, verse 1: "The Lord had said to Abram, 'Leave your country, your people and your father's household and go to the land I will show you.'" It is never easy to move, but this was an especially difficult command for Abraham to obey. He was an old man, 75; he had his roots down deep in the land of Ur. In addition, he was very wealthy: he had many cattle and many servants. It's difficult to transport all of that. But the factor that made it most difficult for Abraham to move was uncertainty. Hebrews 11:8 says, "By faith Abraham, when called to go to a place he would later receive as his inheritance, obeyed and went, even though he did not know where he was going." He was going to move, but he didn't know where he was going!

Where was Sarah, his wife, in all of this negotiation? Genesis 12:5 says "he took his wife" Sarah and his nephew Lot, and they headed for Canaan. I talked to a member of our church some time ago. He had moved to Louisville from the east coast. He had flown here by himself one day; the next day he found a house and bought it; and the next week he brought his wife and children here.

I don't think I'd do that. That would be risky!

Abraham said to Sarah, "We are going to move, but we don't know where we are going." Sarah was affected by this decision, and I am sure she had some input. But the Bible does not say that "God said to Sarah," or even "God said to Abraham and Sarah." It just says, "God said to Abraham, 'I want you to move,'" because God had delegated Abraham to be the leader of this home.

Business schools today are focusing much attention on the difference between management and leadership. Leadership is not being the decision-maker all the time. Leadership is not being the boss where you bark out orders. Leadership is motivating people to develop their skills to the fullest of their potential for the good of the organization. A leader is a person who knows where he is going and is able to persuade others to voluntarily come along.

Abraham didn't know specifically where he was going, but he knew he was following God's will, and he was able to persuade Sarah to go with him. He was a spiritual leader. Hebrews 11:10 says he was looking forward to the city with foundations, whose architect and builder is God.

So men, the first responsibility we have in the marriage is to be the *spiritual leader* of the home.

One man boasted he was the head of the house. He said, "My wife came crawling to me on her hands and knees the other day."

A man who knew him well was startled, and he said, "Really? She came crawling on her hands and knees? What did she say?"

"She said, 'Come out from under that bed and fight like a man!'"

The idea that the man is the leader in the home is not a very popular concept today. But God's Word makes it very clear that he is supposed to be. "Wives, submit to your husbands as to the Lord. For the husband is the head of the wife as Christ is the head of the church" (Ephesians 5:22, 23). Why did God design it that way? Why didn't God say the wife is the head? Why didn't He say it's a fifty/fifty partnership? Why didn't He say take an IQ test and see who is smarter and let that one be the leader? I don't know exactly why God did this, but I can think of a couple of reasons.

One was out of necessity. In order for marriage to be a permanent happy relationship, it was essential that there be a *designated leader*. A football coach designates one player on the field to be the quarterback in the huddle. That is not discrimination; the coach just knows if there is more than one spokesman in the huddle, there is going to be chaos. A corporation does not have a co-presidency because organizational minds know that the slightest disagreement between the two would be divisive and send mixed signals throughout the organization.

Now, the exception to that rule is a business partnership where there is a fifty/fifty investment on the part of two people. But such partnerships have a terrible survival record. It is a structure predisposed to indecision. Neither partner has the authority to prevent a decision from being made, and the partnership stagnates. So wise business counsel advises against entering into a partnership where one person is not ultimately responsible.

When God established the basic building block of society, He didn't create a partnership. He wanted marriage to be permanent, so He appointed a designated leader—out of necessity. The second reason was for fulfillment. God created men in such a way that we are not content if we are not convinced that we are the leader in the home. We men have weak egos. We need to feel that we are in control, and we don't like it when we are not. A man complained that his fishing trip with his wife was a disaster. She did everything wrong. She talked too much. She used the wrong bait. She reeled in too fast, and she caught more fish than he did! We don't like that. We have to feel like we are in control—we are in the lead.

God has constructed women in such a way that they desire the protection of a husband they respect. That is one of the reasons that some of the most intelligent and capable women remain unmarried. Men are intimidated by them. Men have the instinctive feeling to lead, and they shy away from those who make them feel inferior. Most women are not attracted to a man they cannot respect at least as an equal.

The third chapter of Genesis lists the curses that came about because of sin. Man received a curse (verses 17–19); Satan received a curse (verses 14, 15). Listen to this three-fold curse on Eve because of sin (verse 16): "I will greatly increase your pains in childbearing. . . . Your desire will be for your husband, and he will rule over you."

It's a curse to have pain in childbirth, and it's a curse to have your husband rule over you. And what does it mean "your desire will be for your husband"? Scholars continue to debate this expression, but I think it refers to the strange dichotomy that is seen as a woman will sometimes resent somebody with authority over her but, at the same time, experiences an unrest and insecurity if she doesn't feel protection and respect from her husband.

For this system to function as God intended, it's imperative that the man be a Christlike leader, not a dictator. The husband is the head of the wife "as Christ is the head of the church" (Ephesians 5:22). You see, Christ leads by *positive involvement*. He didn't sit in Heaven and bark out commands. Neither did He sit passively in Heaven and do nothing. He took the initiative, came to visit us, and He said, "Follow Me." Husbands, we have a God-given responsibility to set a positive example to be involved, demonstrating compassion, integrity, temperance, ambition, and spirituality.

One of the biggest problems in the home today is the passive male. Many who are business leaders come home and don't want any more responsibility. It's the easiest thing to put your mind in neutral and force the wife to handle everything in the home. I confess, that is a temptation of mine. I have to lead a church every day, and when I come home, I am tired—and I have a most capable wife. She is a great organizer, she has more business ability than I, she is strong-willed, and she is capable of running our home without any input from me. And the temptation for me is to be uninvolved.

We went to see a movie together the other day in which Indians give a soldier a new name. They call him "Dances With Wolves." My wife could give me some new names: "Sits With Paper," "Sleeps on Couch," "Swings at a Ball."

But I have a responsibility from God to take the initiative, help deal with the children, plan the activities, handle the finances, attend the church, and develop the skills in the home. Christ led by positive involvement.

He also led by *self-sacrifice.* "Husbands, love your wives, just as Christ loved the church and gave himself up for her" (Ephesians 5:25). Christ didn't demand His own way. He gave himself up on the cross. If a husband wants to be a Christlike leader, he looks for a way to sacrifice himself for his mate. That means he gives up a night of watching sports, or he gives up some of his money without grumbling, or he gives up a nap to sit at the table and talk with his wife.

And Christ leads by *unconditional love.*

Christ loved the church and gave himself up for her, . . . cleansing her by the washing with water through the word . . . to present her to himself as a radiant church, without stain or wrinkle or any other blemish, but holy and blameless (Ephesians 5:25-27).

Christ does not love us only if we are perfect. His love cleanses us of our sin, and He sees us as without blemish. Husbands have to love their wives just as they are. Even if you think maybe she is too talkative or too heavy or too inhibited, your role, husband, is to love your wife without criticism, without comparing, and without abuse.

Gordon Clinard tells of stopping at a truck stop where he was served by a rather rough-looking waitress who had a tattoo on her arm that said "Charlie." So he struck up a conversation and said, "How's Charlie?"

She said, "Pardon?"

He said, "How's Charlie?"

"Oh," she said. "That. Well, that was years ago and I was high and it was night and—. You know, I haven't seen him since." But then she went on to say, "But you know, I am married to a wonderful man named Richard, and we have been married for ten years, and he is great."

Clinard said, "What does Richard think about Charlie?"

She said, "Oh—you know—from the first time I explained it, he has never mentioned it again. I don't think he even sees it anymore."

That is the way Christ loves the church. He doesn't see our sin anymore. His love covers our sin. And our mates' faults have to be covered and forgotten by love.

Christ leads by *tender kindness*, too. I love that song, "Gentle Shepherd, Lead Us." He doesn't coerce us. He leads us gently.

Look at 1 Peter 3:7: "Husbands, in the same way be considerate as you live with your wives, and treat them with respect as the weaker partner [or "weaker vessel," King James Version] and as heirs with you of the gracious gift of life." Does it sound sexist to you to say, "She is the weaker vessel"? Is that a sexist remark? No. Not at all.

I used this text in a sermon a while back, and to illustrate the point I took two vessels to show to the congregation. I held up the first one and said, "I want to show you this vessel. It's a mug. It has a U of L emblem on the front, but it is a rugged plastic mug. I mean you can beat it around, and you can drop it; it will last for years. You can come up after the service and handle it and punch it if you want to. Even if you scar it—it's only a dollar. This is a strong vessel."

Then I held up a china teacup. I said, "I want to show you another vessel. This is a weaker vessel. It's made out of china from England, and if you were to drop this, it would break. This belongs to my wife. Several years ago, she managed to hint through two or three people that she would like a Laura Ashley Tea Set for Christmas. And if you handle this after the service, handle it with care, because it cost me a bundle. I mean I had to sign my name in blood and wrap it in a towel to bring it here today! This is a weaker vessel. But it's a whole lot more valuable, and you have to treat it with gentleness and consideration. That is what Peter is talking about: husbands, you be considerate with your wives and treat them with respect as the more valuable vessel."

If you are a husband, that means you treat your wife, and you lead, with tenderness and gentleness. You be considerate. You let her off at the front of the church building when it's raining; don't make her park the car. You listen to her attentively when she talks. You put her on a pedestal. You open the car door for her— or at least let her get both legs inside before you take off! You tell her she looks nice. You remember anniversaries. You write a personal note and tell her she is special. You hold her hand. You gently touch her arm. You hug her when you expect nothing in return. You talk to her gently, seldom criticize, and never make fun. Let others see publicly that you love her, and you will be amazed at how responsive she is as you treat her as the more valuable vessel.

Zig Ziglar said if you treat your wife like a thoroughbred, she will seldom act like a nag. Men like the idea of being a leader, but Christ calls us not to a leadership of power, but to a leadership of love. Big difference!

The Wife's Role

Sarah's role was one of a *Christlike responder*. What was Sarah's reaction to Abraham's announcement they were going to move? Did she say, "You've got to be kidding me, old man! You don't know where you are going. I have been here for sixty-five years, and if you think I'm going with you when you don't even know where you're going to land, you've got another thought coming!"

The Old Testament doesn't tell us what Sarah's attitude was. It just says that she went with him. But the New Testament does tell us about her attitude. Look at 1 Peter 3, beginning with verse 3. Talking to the women, Peter said,

> Your beauty should not come from outward adornment. . . . Instead, it should be that of your inner self, the unfading beauty of a gentle

and quiet spirit, which is of great worth in God's sight. For this is the way the holy women of the past who put their hope in God used to make themselves beautiful. They were submissive to their own husbands, like Sarah, who obeyed Abraham and called him her master.

We men don't like the idea of being told we are supposed to be sacrificial; that goes against our carnal nature. And women don't like the idea of being told they are supposed to be submissive; that goes against their carnal nature. But it's important that we understand what it means to be submissive. It does not mean being a doormat. Sarah is cited as the example, but Sarah was no doormat. She was a strong, capable woman who stood up to Abraham and persuaded him to do differently on occasion.

Genesis 21 relates an example. Sarah got irritated because Ishmael, the son of her servant, began to mock her son, Isaac. She said, in Genesis 21:10, "Get rid of that slave woman and her son, for that slave woman's son will never share in the inheritance with my son Isaac."

Does that sound like one who "called him her master"? That's who it is. Nor did Abraham say, "Stifle it, woman. I'm in charge." The next verse reads, "The matter distressed Abraham greatly because it concerned his son." (The servant's son was his son, too.) Then God came to Abraham and said, "You listen to your wife; she is telling you the truth. Hagar and Ishmael need to go" (cf. Genesis 21:12, 13).

You see, to submit does not mean to be a doormat. To submit can mean to make a contribution. When we submit a bid on a house, we present an offer. This is what I am willing to give for that house. To submit sometimes means a willingness to share my resources.

Several years ago, I was preaching on Jacob, who had a number of children by his two wives and two concubines. I flippantly said, "You know, I have always loved big families, and I think, if I had to do it again, I would have six or eight children." Then I remembered that, after our second child, Judy had said, "Never again!" So I said, "Of course, if I did that, I would have to have a concubine or two—Ha, Ha, Ha!"

After the first service, I was standing in the hallway greeting people as they went through. My wife was standing beside me, and when there was a lull in the conversation, she said, "I wouldn't use that line about a concubine in the next service if I were you." You see, she submitted an idea. And I bought it! I thought it was a very good submission, and I changed.

To be submissive, then, doesn't mean you are a wimp or a whipped puppy. Submission does mean that we acknowledge and respect God's delegated line of authority. If I rebel against the law of my country, I am rebelling against the authority that has been delegated by God. I can express disagreement. I can try to change the law, but I have a responsibility to be submissive to the law of the land because the law has been appointed by God. The only time I have a right to resist the government is when the government asks me to do something that is contrary to what God's Word says.

If a wife rebels against her husband's leadership, she is rebelling against God's delegated line of authority. She has a right to express disagreement and seek to persuade change, but if the husband is insistent, then she has a responsibility, like Sarah, to be cooperative. The only time she has a right to resist is when he asks her to do something that is contrary to God's Word. For example, if he's beating the children and he tells her not to interfere, or if he forbids her to give spiritual training to the children, or if he asks her to do something that is perverted. Obviously, it is much easier for the wife to submit if the husband is a Christlike leader, but 1 Peter 3 says a wife should be submissive even if the husband is not a believer—so he will be won over by the demonstration of her life. (See 1 Peter 3:1, 2.)

A key phrase here is that the wife is to be a *Christlike* responder. How did Christ respond? Look at Philippians 2, beginning with verse 5. It says:

Your attitude should be the same as that of Christ Jesus: Who, being in very nature God, did not consider equality with God something to be grasped, but he made himself nothing, taking the very nature of a servant, being made in human likeness. And being found in appearance

as a man, he humbled himself and became obedient to death—even
death on a cross!

How did Christ respond? He responded *voluntarily*. He was
equal with God. He was the one who created the world. But He
humbled himself to God's will and became obedient to the
Father's wishes, even to the point of dying on the cross. He took
that subservient role temporarily so that the human race could
be saved. For a wife to be submissive does not mean she is inferior. Like Jesus Christ, she voluntarily accepts the assignment for
the salvation of the family. She can stubbornly resist, insist on
her rights, and keep her pride. But I will guarantee you the
family suffers.

By the way, God does not say women are to be submissive to
men. It doesn't say that. In the Bible there are women judges,
there are women rulers, there are women who are in business. It
just says that in the sphere of the family and the church family,
the man is to be the acknowledged leader.

Jesus submitted himself voluntarily. He also submitted himself
joyfully. Hebrews 12:2: "Let us fix our eyes on Jesus, . . . who for
the joy set before him endured the cross." Jesus didn't grumble
and complain about going to the cross. He went joyfully,
knowing that He was being obedient to the Father. Sometimes a
Christian woman will be submissive, but will do so with a
grudging, bitter spirit. There should be a spirit of joy. We are
walking in the steps of Christ.

Finally, Jesus submitted *with honor*. "Therefore God exalted
him to the highest place and gave him the name that is above
every name" (Philippians 2:9). Far from being degrading, we
honor Christ because He was submissive. We say, "Wow! He even
washed feet." We sing, "In the cross of Christ I glory." It is not degrading for a wife to have a compliant spirit. It is to her honor.

Almost all Americans know the name of General Norman
Schwarzkopf, the commander of U.S. forces in Operation Desert
Storm. Schwarzkopf came home a hero because of his accom-
plishments in the Persian Gulf, and he had the media's attention
for weeks. Disappointed that Iraq's President Sadaam Hussein

had not been ousted by his people after his stunning defeat, Schwarzkopf made a comment that maybe we should have stayed a couple of days longer in Iraq. The media picked that up and left the impression that there was a division between the President and the General. So Schwarzkopf sent a memo to President Bush saying, "I apologize if I said anything that would bring an embarrassment to the Presidency." It wasn't a condescending apology, but a humble one.

General Schwarzkopf may have been right, and he may have been in a better position than the President to make that decision, and he may be more intelligent than the President, but none of that matters! He acknowledged the line of military authority. He knew the President was his Commander in Chief. Personally, the fact that he made an apology only enhances my respect for him. He could have become defensive; he could have taken advantage of his popularity. Instead, he acknowledged where the line of authority was, and he was answerable to the Commander in Chief.

Far from being degrading, a compliant, submissive spirit to God's delegated authority is a tribute to your understanding that Jesus Christ is your Commander in Chief.

I met an interesting couple in Lansing, Michigan, a few years back. They had met in Milwaukee, where the woman, perhaps the sharper of the two, had a wonderful executive position with a large corporation. She was making a lot more money than her husband, who worked for an insurance agency. Both of them were over forty when they married, not a good age for either one to try to change jobs. Six months into their marriage, however, the husband got transferred for a promotion. He tried every way out, but there was no alternative. He finally said to his wife, "Honey, I want to take this promotion. I know I could quit and try to find something else and we could live off your salary, but for my self-worth I would like to take this job."

She was then faced with a decision as to whether she would leave her career for her marriage, or whether she would tell her husband she was not going and put the ball in his court. She made a decision that she would go with him and move to

Lansing. She found another job there, though it was not nearly as lucrative as her previous one. I talked with them two years later, and she said, "You know, when I got married, I knew that Bill had to be more important than anything else, and we are so happy in our marriage." And then she said, "It was well worth the price; he has me on an incredible pedestal."

You can say she was a fool—I'm sure some people did tell her that. I rather think she is an obedient, loving servant of God. You see, God has made us very different. We have different roles. But I have observed, when the man is a Christlike leader and the woman is a Christlike responder, the issue of who has the authority is hardly ever discussed. It's not important. Both are submitting and both are being unselfish to the other. When they don't acknowledge that role, and they dig in their heels, the marriage is a constant tug of war to see who is really in charge.

God knew what He was doing when He designed marriage. It's just a matter of our being submissive to His delegated authority and confessing Jesus Christ above all.

3

LEARN TO LOVE

(ISAAC AND REBEKAH)

"I just don't love you anymore." Pat Williams, who at the time was the general manager of the Philadelphia 76er's basketball team, was startled when he heard his wife, Jill, speak those words. She sat straight up in bed and said, "Of all the places in the world, I would rather be anyplace else but here. I will stay with you for the sake of image," she said, "but my love is dead."

Pat woke up to the fact that his wife had been neglected to the point that she did not feel anything for him anymore. Publicly, they had it all. She had been a beauty queen and was an outstanding violinist; he was part owner of a professional basketball team. But now the most important part of his life was a failure.

Pat Williams set out to try to win his wife back. He was determined to prove to her that she was important to him and that he did love her. Reluctantly, she agreed to try. At the time, the Williams were nominal church members, but that disturbance in their marriage drove them into a deeper relationship with the Lord. Instead of saying, "If there is no feeling, there is no marriage," they began to rebuild.

Pat and Jill Williams wrote about their experience and how love was restored in their marriage in a book I would recommend for you. It's entitled simply *Rekindled*. A subtitle on the cover of the book promises, "How to keep the warmth in marriage."

Is that really possible? Is it possible for a dead love to be resurrected? If the flames of passion have gone out, can they ever be rekindled? Can a person really force himself to love somebody if he doesn't feel anything?

We have a difficult time with this idea, because "love American style" has been so romanticized. From the time we are little, we dream about meeting somebody who will melt our hearts and fulfill our fantasies. In fact, we are told, "God has somebody out there for you who will be the right one. When you meet that person, you will fall in love and it will be forever." So we spend our high school years—maybe our college years—searching for that special feeling. Maybe you have come home from a date and said, "I really believe this is the one!" Then several days later you found yourself saying, "Oh, no! He chewed with his mouth open; he's not the right one."

When you reach your early twenties, you might find somebody that you really care about. He might not quite measure up to your expectations; he doesn't make your heart beat fast all the time. But you feel comfortable with him, and you feel lonely without him, and you begin to ask yourself, "Do I love this person enough to spend the rest of my life with him? Is my feeling for him great enough to be committed to him, or will I find somebody else I can love more?"

A song that was popular several years ago mourned, "Oh, it's sad to belong to someone else when the right one comes along." Too many people feel time is running out and options seem to be few, so they agree to get married, hoping that the love they feel will intensify with time. Sadly, the feelings diminish.

Somebody has said the cycle of married love goes from romance to reality to resentment to rebellion. In order to avoid that cycle of disillusionment, we need some Biblical instruction about learning to love. The Bible makes it clear that God never intended marriage to be based on something as unstable, unpredictable, and uncontrollable as a loving *feeling*. There is love in marriage, but it bears little resemblance to the Hollywood image of romantic love about which we fantasize.

Let's look at the story of Isaac and Rebekah to learn some very important truths about love in marriage. Some of you desperately need to learn these truths. If you will dare to believe in them and plug into them, these basic principles can save your marriage and rekindle real love in your home.

The story of Isaac and Rebekah is contained in Genesis, the twenty-fourth chapter. Abraham decided that it was time for his son to marry, so he gave his servant an assignment. Verse 4: "Go to my country and my own relatives and get a wife for my son, Isaac." In that culture, young people did not date and make their own selection based on romance. The parents made the selection based on practical matters like compatibility, financial status, and religious beliefs.

Abraham told his servant there were two qualifications. First, he must find a wife for Isaac from his homeland. Number 2, she must be willing to relocate. She had to be willing to come to Canaan because that was the land God had given to him and his descendants.

The servant then headed for Ur of the Chaldees, leading a caravan of servants and ten camels and taking with him a number of gifts. He stopped at a watering hole outside the town of Nahor and asked God for guidance.

Have you ever arranged a blind date for somebody? It really puts the pressure on you because you are afraid that you are going to make a wrong selection and both people are going to be angry with you. This servant was not just arranging a blind date —he was arranging a blind marriage! The pressure was really on. So he did what most of us would do in that situation: he asked God for guidance. "O Lord, be kind to my master, Abraham. Help me to be a success on this mission. Give me a sign to know which girl I'm supposed to select" (cf. Genesis 24:12).

See, I am standing beside this spring, and the daughters of the townspeople are coming out to draw water. May it be that when I say to a girl, "Please let down your jar that I may have a drink," and she says, "Drink, and I'll water your camels too"—let her be the one you have chosen for your servant Isaac (Genesis 24:13, 14).

I read that a thirsty camel can drink thirty gallons of water, and there were ten camels here. If any woman would say, "Let me draw 300 gallons of water for your camels," that was going to be a special sign from the Lord—I will guarantee you!

As soon as He finished his prayer—in fact, verse 15 says *before* he finished praying—Rebekah came out with her jar on her shoulder. Perhaps if we would just follow the criteria that God used for selecting a mate for Isaac, it would help us in taking the risk out of mate selection, and it would help us to choose somebody who would be easier to love.

Criteria for Choosing a Mate

Rebekah was an *energetic worker*. She regularly carried water to supply her household. And she had a *similar background* to Isaac: verse 15 says she was a distant relative. According to verse 16, she was very beautiful. She had an *attractive appearance*, and that would please Isaac. I read that men usually choose beauty over brains because most men see better than they think! Rebekah was not only beautiful on the outside, she was attractive within. Verse 16 says she was "a virgin; no man had ever lain with her." She had *moral purity*.

Above all this, however, maybe one of the most outstanding qualities about Rebekah was that she had a *congenial personality*. Look at verses 17 through 20:

> The servant hurried to meet her and said, "Please give me a little water from your jar."
>
> "Drink, my lord," she said, and quickly lowered the jar to her hands and gave him a drink.
>
> After she had given him a drink, she said, "I'll draw water for your camels too [There's the sign!], until they have finished drinking." So she quickly emptied her jar into the trough, ran back to the well to draw more water, and drew enough for all his camels.

You can see right away that Rebekah has a congenial, cooperative personality. If you have a mate who is volatile and unpredictable, one who makes you walk on eggshells all the time, it's more difficult to love. One of the most important characteristics in a partner is somebody who is easy to live with.

Rebekah also had a *spiritual maturity,* which is made evident a little later as the story develops. But this servant was so pleased that here was a girl who watered his camels and was obviously God's choice that he began to give her gifts. He gave her two gold bracelets and a gold nose ring. Well, that will do it every time! I don't know what a gold nose ring was, but she was pleased with it.

"Whose daughter are you?" the servant asked excitedly. "I must speak with your father" (cf. Genesis 24:23). Then he bowed down and worshiped the Lord for His goodness (Genesis 24:26).

Rebekah ran home to tell her family what had happened, and her brother Laban came out to see what was going on at the well. When he saw this servant with all these expensive gifts, he said, "We want you to come to our house. We have room for your camels. You must have a meal with us."

The servant went to Laban's home and met Rebekah's father, Bethuel. Before they even ate a meal, he had to explain his mission. "I came to find a wife for my master, Isaac," he said, "and I prayed that the good Lord would give me a sign, and Rebekah has fulfilled the sign."

Laban and Bethuel answered, "The Lord has obviously brought you here, so what can we say? Take her and go. Yes, let her be the wife of your master's son as Jehovah has directed."

The next day, the servant was ready to go, but Rebekah's family hesitated. "Oh, wait a minute! Not so fast!" they said. "Why don't we give her ten days or so to say good-bye and get the house in order?"

But the servant said, "Please don't detain me. My master has sent me on a mission; let me leave with Rebekah immediately."

They said, "Let's call the girl and ask her about it."

And Rebekah said, "I will go now."

Rebekah had to be very special. Not only was she sensitive to doing God's will immediately, but any woman who could pack in one day without any advance notice had to be really special!

Where Does Love Come In?

They took off. Rebekah was heading to a new land to marry a man she had never met. Verse 63 relates Isaac's reaction to

Rebekah. He went out in the field one evening to meditate. He must have been wondering what God had in store. Then, as He looked up, he saw camels approaching. I think his heart began to pound, wondering whether his wife-to-be was in that caravan, and he ran to meet it.

Rebekah also looked up and saw Isaac. She got down from her camel and asked the servant, "Who is that man in the field coming to meet us?"

"He is my master," the servant answered. "That is the one you are going to marry."

So she took her veil and covered herself. Evidently Isaac didn't even get to see Rebekah until after they were married—didn't even get to see her face. Can you imagine that? That is so foreign to our way of thinking!

The servant told Isaac all that he had done. Now, the final verse of this chapter is the key verse:

> Isaac brought her into the tent of his mother Sarah, and he married Rebekah. So she became his wife, and he loved her; and Isaac was comforted after his mother's death (Genesis 24:67).

Notice the sequence of that final verse again. It doesn't say Isaac dated Rebekah and fell in love with her and then they got married based on romance. It says he brought her into the tent of his mother and he married her. She became his wife, and *then* he loved her. That is a different sequence altogether.

Here is the principle that I want to draw out of this story. Love is an act of the will. It is more than just an emotion of the heart. Romantic love is the *result* of a right relationship. It is not the *basis* of it. There is a big difference between the world's concept of love and the Biblical teaching about love. Our world considers love an involuntary emotion: it's something you fall into as you might fall into a ditch. We have had those songs for decades: "Some enchanted evening, across a crowded room you will meet a stranger, and your world will never be the same again!" Elvis sang, "I can't help falling in love with you." The Righteous Brothers sang, "You've lost that loving feeling," and the rock group The Doors sang, "Hello, I love you, won't you tell me your name." The Young Cannibals have a song that says, "She drives me crazy, and I can't help myself." There is certainly an emotional experience called infatuation. You can be very physically or emotionally attracted to somebody. The chemistry is right between you; your heart pounds, your breathing accelerates, and your knees wobble. Your mind focuses on that person exclusively, and there is an emotional turbulence. You say, "Oh, boy! This is it. I've found *love!*"

Norman Wright terms that "cardiac respiratory love." Scott Peck calls it a genetic trick that nature plays on us to get two people together to learn real love.

Whatever you call it, infatuation always wears off. Those feelings are always temporary. If you expect that emotional experience to last or to intensify in marriage, you are going to be deeply disappointed. In fact, the more intense the infatuation, the more precarious the marriage relationship will be.

I have counseled with a number of couples before they got married. Sometimes I ask them, "What is there about your partner that irritates you the most?" If they say, "Oh, I just can't think of anything I don't like about him. I love him so much—I just love everything!" then I will think to myself, "Boy, you are in for a rude awakening." I want to say, "See me in about two years." (She'd have a list by then, you know!)

Infatuation does not last. It's not the primary basis of marital love. You can be infatuated with somebody who would make a terrible married partner. You can be infatuated with somebody who doesn't even know you. You can be happily married and all of a sudden the chemistry is right between you and somebody else, but that is not a reason to have an affair or get a divorce. It's just a reason to be smart and say, "Ah, this too will pass."

The Bible speaks of something deeper, more stable, than infatuation. It speaks of *agape* love. That is deeper than *eros*, erotic love. *Agape* means to give yourself to another regardless of feeling, to do the right thing regardless of feeling. That kind of love is an act of the will. It is not an uncontrollable emotion; it is a decision of the mind: "I will give myself to this person."

The most tender scene in *Fiddler on the Roof* is where Tevye, on the night of his daughter's marriage, asks his wife of twenty-five years, "Do you love me?" Their marriage had been arranged, and, as Tevye explains to his wife, "My mother and father said we would learn to love each other. And now, I am asking you, Golde, do you love me?"

She begins to recount some of the loving experiences that they have had over the years, and finally she says, "I suppose I do." Agape love: giving yourself, learning to care.

Rekindling Love

There are two reasons that I believe we can learn to love. First, the Bible commands us to love each other. "Husbands, love your wives," it says. God would never require of us something that we could not control, would He?

The second reason is that I know of thousands of couples who have done it—even couples who once thought their feelings were dead, but they have been resurrected, and their love has been rekindled.

Jim Whitworth is an elder in our church. A couple of years ago, he stood up and related how, a decade before, he and his wife were on the verge of getting a divorce. Their feelings were gone, he said, but they counseled with a Christian who said, "Even though you are not happy, remember, God has not called you to be happy. God has called you to be obedient." And they walked out of the counseling session and recommitted themselves to their marriage. They rekindled love.

I was in their home recently, a beautiful new house. They have love, joy, children who are pleased that they stayed together, and a God who is pleased that they have stayed together. Don't tell me it can't be done! I sincerely believe that no matter how badly you have been hurt, how dead you think your feelings are, God can resurrect your situation if you will cooperate with His will.

If a Christian husband and wife will both determine to love, God can restore their love—sometimes in a brief period of time. It takes both partners working together. If you are in a situation where you want to rekindle love and your mate does not, that is a different situation. (The next chapter talks about handling conflict in marriage.) But if there is a Christian couple who wants to restore love to their marriage, they can do it.

I want to close out this chapter by giving you seven things that you can do if you really want to rekindle love in your marriage or to keep the warmth in your marriage. Don't say it's impossible until you try them.

Number one, *make a commitment to your partner exclusively.* Winston Churchill rallied England during World War II with the phrase, "Wars are not won by evacuations." Marriages are not kept together by bailing out. So don't be looking around wondering whether somebody else is available for romance. Renew your commitment to your partner. Maybe go back and listen to the tape recording of your ceremony again, especially the part where you said, "For better, for worse, for richer or for poorer, in sickness and in health." (That is not multiple choice!)

Charles Swindoll said the grass may look greener on the other side of the fence, but it's always poison. God put the fence there for a reason. Recommit yourself to your partner exclusively. Don't look back.

Second, *pray for God's power to transform your feelings.* Look at Genesis 25:21: "Isaac prayed to the Lord on behalf of his wife, because she was barren. The Lord answered his prayer, and his wife Rebekah became pregnant." In fact, she became pregnant with twins! Make a vow that you will pray every day that God will change your barren feelings. Pray specifically, "God help me to release my hostility and replace it with Your compassion." Then begin to pray that God will resurrect the barren feelings in your partner. Prayer not only releases God's healing power in your marriage. It forces you to swallow your pride and humble yourself before Him.

If you dare, the two of you pray together. You will be amazed how much of a difference that will make in rekindling your love. Ephesians 3:20 says God is able to do immeasurably more than all we ask or imagine, according to His power that is at work in us.

The third step, perhaps the most difficult, is to *dedicate your-self to fulfilling your mate's needs* instead of focusing on your own unmet needs. Focus on your mate's needs. When love is dormant in a marriage, each partner wallows in self-pity. "Oh, he won't encourage me." "She won't reinforce me." But, if you really want to restore love, forget your needs and focus completely on the desires of your mate. That means you become unselfish, make yourself vulnerable, and focus on the other's desires, even if it's not coming out even. You don't keep score and say, "Well, you know, I took her out to eat and gave her a nice evening, and her attitude has not changed—it's just a one-way street, and that is it!" You just sacrifice yourself; forget yourself and become involved in providing for your mate's happiness.

Mike and Kathy, a couple from our church, gave a moving testimony about the transformation in their marriage. They told how, three years earlier, their marriage was dead and they were on the way to divorce court when they decided to turn it around. They both gave their lives to Christ. One of the ways that they rekindled their love was that they both decided to do something for the other that would meet their needs.

Kathy loved ballroom dancing, and Mike was humiliated to dance. So when they got back together, he secretly signed up for ten Arthur Murray dance lessons. His friends were shocked. He said on about the fifth lesson, they had an odd number there, so he got paired with some man, and he said, "That's it!" He went and got his wife and brought her in and he learned to dance with her. That was not what he wanted to do, but he did it for her.

Kathy decided she would take up golf—not because she wanted to play golf, but because Mike loved to play golf. And she asked her instructor, "Do I need a new swing?" and he said, "You need a new sport!" That was not what she wanted to do, but she did that for him. Somehow it helped to rekindle love when they began to try to meet the other's needs.

You might say, "Boy, if I did that, my life would be miserable." No. Your life would be fulfilled. Jesus said, if you seek to save your life, you are going to lose it. But if you lose your life for His sake and the gospel's, you will find it.

Let me remind you: if you are a parent, you have already done that, and it works. You brought that little baby home from the hospital, and he could not meet any of your needs, but you focused yourself entirely on meeting that baby's needs. You got the bottle in the middle of the night, and you changed diapers at inopportune times, and you paid money for doctor bills. After that child was six months old, he still wasn't doing anything for you, but you were so madly in love with that child you would do anything for him. When you focus on meeting another's needs and you sacrifice for that person, you fall in love with him.

That is the reason Jesus said if you have an enemy and he is hungry, feed him. If he is thirsty, give him something to drink. Why? You'll learn to love him.

Fourth: *Deliberately act the way you wish you felt*. If you act the way you wish you felt, you will eventually feel the way you act. If you allow your emotions to dictate your life, you are vulnerable to all kinds of instability and perverted activity. But if you do what you know you should do, regardless of how you feel, eventually your feelings will change. That is not hypocrisy; that is obedience.

I took a golf lesson once, and the instructor said, "I'll tell you what you have to do: you've got to change your grip. Your grip is too strong. Turn your wrist over here."

I said, "Boy, that feels awkward."

He said, "I don't care how it feels. That is the right way. You just keep practicing that way and eventually it will feel right. And if you don't do it that way, you are never going to be able to hit the ball consistently."

With all respect to your situation, I don't care how you feel; there is a right way to do it. It's God's way. You make a commitment, "I'm going to act the way I wish I felt." It is much easier to act yourself into the right way of feeling than it is to feel yourself into the right way of acting.

Fifth: *spend time together, just the two of you*. When my wife and I were dating, we spent a lot of time, just the two of us, talking and listening. Part of the reason, to be honest, was that we didn't have enough money to go out for entertainment, so we just talked and listened. "Tell me again what you did in 4H, that was so interesting." Well. . . . But we got to know each other. Then, when we got married, I was focusing on a new ministry, she was in a full-time job, and we weren't communicating very much. Our salvation was that about every three months we would take a long trip—three hours—to visit her parents, or a seven-hour trip to visit my parents, and all of a sudden we had to talk again. There she was, just two feet from me, no newspaper to read, no television to watch, no sleep available, and slowly the barriers would break down and we would talk and rekindle love.

Somebody said that communication is to a relationship what oxygen is to your body. In fact, to this day, if I will say to Judy, "Hey, we have got a Friday night free this week; what do you want to do? Go out and eat, go to a movie? Go out and eat and go to a ball game? Go out and eat and go to this—" she almost always will say, "Let's just go out and eat," and I know what she wants. Get in a restaurant all by ourselves for an hour or two and, after we eat, just sit and talk. That is romance.

Some couples never spend any time alone anymore. Why? They say they are bored, or it just hurts—it's too much work to talk, so they always get other couples with them, or always have the kids as an excuse. If you have to, take a long drive together, but somehow go someplace by yourselves regularly where you are alone.

Sixth: *restore sexual intimacy to your marriage right now*. Genesis 26:8 relates that when Isaac and Rebekah were visiting Gerar, "Abimelech king of the Philistines looked out at a window, and saw, and, behold, Isaac was sporting with Rebekah." That is the King James Version: "Isaac was *sporting* with Rebekah." That is the oldest sport in the world! The New International Version says, "Isaac was caressing Rebekah." God endorsed that.

When couples drift apart, sometimes they will say, "Well, you know, if we can get it together emotionally and we can get together communication-wise, and I feel good about the relationship, then we will get it together sexually." No! No! No! Restore sexual intimacy in your marriage right now. That is God's will for you. Look at 1 Corinthians 7:3–5:

The husband should fulfill his marital duty to his wife, and likewise the wife to her husband. The wife's body does not belong to her alone but also to her husband. In the same way, the husband's body does not belong to him alone but also to his wife. Do not deprive each other except by mutual consent and for a time. . . . Then come together again so that Satan will not tempt you because of your lack of self-control.

When you are on a diet, how often do you get hungry? All the time! If you don't have affection in your marriage, you are sending a partner out there who is starved for affection and vulnerable to temptation. So it is God's will that there be regular physical expressions of love in marriage. I want to say to you as tenderly as I can say it, if you are sleeping on the couch and your mate is sleeping in the bedroom—or if there is no caressing or physical intimacy even though you sleep in the same bed—you are outside God's will. You can pretend you are just being pious, but I suggest to you, somebody in that relationship is very, very selfish. You get it together. "May you rejoice in the wife of your youth. . . . May her breasts satisfy you always, may you ever be captivated by her love" (Proverbs 5:18, 19). That is God's will.

The greatest love stories are not the ones you see in a movie. The greatest love stories take place in places you never see with godly couples who have learned to express their affection to one another in the way God intended.

The last step is to *develop spiritual maturity*. Jesus said if you will seek first the kingdom of God and His righteousness, all these things will be added to you (Matthew 6:33). If two Christian people will really surrender their lives to Jesus Christ and then to each other, He will bring them together—I guarantee it. That means you go to church regularly, and you sit with each other; you hold hands when you say grace at the table; you talk about your spiritual values, and you make a commitment to grow in Jesus Christ. It means there is no sin or past failure that can't be forgotten, there is no wound that can't be healed, there is no flaw that can't be overlooked, and there is no buried love that can't be resurrected. But it does require a growing toward Jesus Christ and a submission of your will to the authority of God.

Remember when Jesus met a man by the pool of Bethesda? The man had been sick for thirty-eight years. Jesus asked him a strange question. He said, "Do you want to get well?" Some of you have had unhealthy relationships for a long time; let me ask you, do you want to get well? Or would you rather just wallow in self-pity and maybe look for an excuse to test the poison grass on the other side of the fence?

Do you want to get well? Then why don't you begin today? Surrender your life first of all to Jesus and then to your mate.

Jill Williams sat up in bed and said, "I would rather be any place in the world than right here," but she and Pat agreed to try to rekindle romance. Two years later, she wrote him a note, addressed to "the greatest husband in the world." Almost two years to the day after they had that first confrontation, they adopted two oriental children in their home in addition to the children they already had. And Jill wrote Pat this note:

Dear Pat,

 I love you so much for your response to that darkest hour two years ago today, and a large part of that response encompasses two oriental dolls sleeping upstairs tonight. That you would share your name, life and love with them is beyond their understanding. That you would share your name, life, love and yourself with me is truly my dream come true. There aren't enough words to express my love and devotion to you. I am the most blessed of all women.

Love Jill[4]

It can be rekindled—agape love—if you want to get well. Jesus shared His life and His love with you by giving himself completely on the cross. Surrender your life back to Him. Let Him rekindle the love in your marriage.

---

[4]Pat and Jill Williams, *Rekindled* (Old Tappan: Revell, 1985).

4

RESOLVE CONFLICT

(JACOB AND RACHEL)

If Prince Charles and Princess Diana are suffering from irreconcilable differences, what should they do? That was a question *People* magazine asked thousands of readers in its tenth annual "Readers Opinion Poll" some time ago. Thirty-seven percent said Charles and Diana should get a divorce and give up once and for all. Sixteen percent suggested the royal couple should suffer quietly, "like the rest of us." Nine percent said the couple should "take lovers and keep up appearances for the sake of propriety." Thirty-four percent said they should "put on Frank Sinatra records, drink some wine and hope for the best." In other words, try to rekindle some affection.

How do you handle the differences that surface in marriage relationships? Do you run away, tough it out, cheat on your mate, complain constantly, or what?

Conflicts are an inevitable part of every marriage. There is a sense in which every couple has irreconcilable differences. I asked a young couple who were married a year ago to write down some of the difficulties they experienced their first year of marriage. Both husband and wife are lawyers. They are Christians, well-suited for each other, and very much in love, but there have been conflicts.

The husband wrote,

Although we were engaged for nearly a year, the transition to married life has not necessarily been a smooth transition. Our personality

51

differences often provided opportunities for conflict rather than harmony. It seemed at times that every conversation would turn into a
confrontation. For the most part, the frequent confrontations would
not discourage me because I believed them to demonstrate that we
were attempting to communicate. I had been told that those couples
who look for ways to avoid conflict for the sake of harmony only tend
to give up on the marriage in later years when the same conflicts continue or resurface. . . .

Our confrontations followed a similar pattern no matter what the
subject. As soon as a point of confrontation was reached, I was overcome with the feeling that I must hold my ground and not give in to
her because if I did I would be giving up something I thought was
right, reasonable, or fair. As I gripped this feeling, the confrontation
would escalate or we would not speak to each other for a brief time.
Finally I would look to the "big picture," which is how much I love
Jennifer, and initiate a reconciliation, usually by apologizing.

I believe with patience and God's guidance, these conflicts will
continue to reduce in number until we have completely adjusted to
married life. In order to get there, I will have to learn how to talk in
a gentle manner with Jennifer. Probably her two most frequent
complaints are that I speak to her in a harsh tone when I disagree
or am critical of her behavior and that I don't pay enough attention
to her.

Mature, talented, Christian couples are not exempt from conflict. And the differences don't automatically dissolve with time.
Many happy couples learn to leave some things unsaid and avoid
some subjects altogether because they know those issues will
never be resolved. Other issues, however, must be faced and an
understanding reached in order for the relationship to continue
in harmony.

It's been said that marriages go through three stages: "The
Happy Honeymoon," "The Party's Over," and "Let's Make a Deal."

I've read that John Wesley and his wife didn't always get along.
She sat in City Road Chapel and made faces at him while he
preached. Some suggest their relationship was a prime motiva-
tion for his becoming a circuit riding preacher!

Jacob and his wife Rachel had a stormy relationship. They loved each other, but their marriage encountered frequent difficulty. Even though they didn't always handle it well, their experience can serve to teach us some lessons about how to handle conflict in marriage.

Some Reasons for Conflict

In-Laws. One of the reasons for Jacob and Rachel's problem was Laban—Jacob's father-in-law. Jacob fell in love with Rachel at first sight. After a few weeks, he asked her father for Rachel's hand in marriage. Laban took advantage of the situation and demanded that Jacob work seven years for the privilege of marrying his daughter.

The Bible says that those seven years seemed but a few days because he was so much in love with her. What a love story! One expects the next line to be, "and they lived happily ever after." But not so.

On the night of the wedding, Laban pulled a cruel trick on both Jacob and Rachel. His devious plan would accomplish two things; marry off his older, less attractive daughter, Leah, and secure the services of Jacob for another seven years.

"Now Laban had two daughters; the name of the older was Leah, and the name of the younger was Rachel. Leah had weak eyes, but Rachel was lovely in form, and beautiful" (Genesis 29:16, 17). Rachel was extremely attractive, but apparently Leah was not. "When evening came, [Laban] took his daughter Leah and gave her to Jacob, and Jacob lay with her" (Genesis 29:23).

Jacob married the wrong girl! Perhaps Leah wore a heavy veil and the ceremony was at night. I wouldn't be surprised if Laban didn't go so far as to spike the punch bowl at the reception. However Laban orchestrated, Jacob somehow married Leah without knowing it, and Rachel was restrained and could do nothing about it.

Imagine Jacob's horror the next morning when, in the daylight, he rolled over and there beside him was Leah! At first he must have wiped the sleep from his eyes and thought, "You know, my mother told me that women don't look nearly as good in the morning, but this is absurd!" Then it hit him: "This isn't Rachel! Why it's—Leah!"

Jacob bolted out of the tent in a rage. When he found his father-in-law, he demanded an explanation. Laban was prepared for Jacob's tantrum. He calmly said, "Look, it's our custom for the older daughter to be married first. That's just our way. You are a lucky man, Jacob, you can marry both my daughters. You can have Rachel, too, if you'll just work seven more years for me." Jacob, who had been a master deceiver himself (impersonating his brother and manipulating his father) was now the victim of deceit. He had no recourse but to agree.

Jacob was able to marry Rachel, but his marriage started off on a sour note because of interference from his father-in-law. That's a common source of conflict today. How often do we visit? How much interference and/or manipulation do we permit? Do we borrow money or accept large cash gifts? Will we invite one of the parents to live with us? A poor relationship with in-laws can be a constant source of conflict.

Spiritual Differences. Another underlying difficulty for Jacob and Rachel came as a result of their religious differences. Jacob had been reared to worship Jehovah. Rachel was accustomed to idol worship. (See Genesis 31:19, 34.) Not much is said in Scripture about their spiritual differences, but it must have created stress. The Bible warns us, "Do not be yoked together with unbelievers. For what do righteousness and wickedness have in common? Or what fellowship can light have with darkness?" (2 Corinthians 6:14).

I frequently get letters from people who are struggling with major problems: affairs, incest, wife-beating, alcohol, mistrust, and constant unhappiness. I hurt for those who want to be true to the Lord but are married to someone who has no commitment to Christ at all. They are in situations that seem impossible to resolve. Someone said, "If you're a child of God and you marry a child of the devil, you're certain to have trouble with your father-in-law." It takes an extra measure of patience and prayer to remain faithful to the Lord while living with a mate who is hostile to Biblical values.

When we deviate from God's plan for marriage, we reap a bitter harvest. Abigail Van Buren received a letter that read, "Dear Abby, I'm in love and I am having an affair with two different women. I can't marry them both. Please tell me what to do, but don't give me any of that morality stuff."

Abby's reply was a classic: "Dear sir, The only difference between humans and animals is morality. I suggest you write your veterinarian."

When we deviate from God's plan, we live like animals, and we can expect trouble. Jacob was in for a lifelong conflict—he was married to two women who did not share his faith.

Feeling Unloved. Jacob did not love Leah, and yet she was his wife and his responsibility.

> When the Lord saw that Leah was not loved, He opened her womb, but Rachel was barren. Leah became pregnant and gave birth to a son. She named him Reuben, for she said, "he has seen my misery" (Genesis 29:31, 32).

Leah thought, "Surely Jacob will love me now!" But there was not much change in his attitude. Children enhance a good marriage, but they underscore problems in a bad one. Leah "conceived again, and when she gave birth to a son she said, "'Because the Lord heard that I am not loved, he gave me this one too'" (Genesis 29:33).

After the birth of their third son, Leah said, "Now at last my husband will become attached to me" (Genesis 29:34). Still no change. After the sixth son she said, "This time my husband will treat me with honor" (Genesis 30:20). What a sad verse! It's a terrible experience to feel unloved by the one who is your lifelong partner. There are many spouses like Leah who would do almost anything for their mates if only for a minute they could believe that they were loved!

Mother Teresa has said that loneliness and the feeling of being unloved are the greatest poverty. There are husbands and wives living in material wealth and abundance who are emotionally poor because they feel unloved. They beg their mates verbally and non-verbally, "Show me that you care!" Loneliness is a frequent source of conflict in marriage.

Infertility. While Leah felt the pain of being unloved, Rachel felt the pain of infertility. Psalm 127:3–5 reads:

> Sons are a heritage from the Lord, children a reward from him. Like arrows in the hands of a warrior are sons born in one's youth. Blessed is the man whose quiver is full of them.

Rachel was loved, but she was barren. That was a dreadful curse in that day. "When Rachel saw that she was not bearing Jacob any children, she became jealous of her sister. So she said to Jacob, 'Give me children, or I'll die!'" (Genesis 30:1).

Studies reveal that infertility affects fifteen percent of our population. Couples who want children can become angry with God and irritable with one another. One woman who could not have children wrote to me concerning her frustration.

> No one expects to be infertile. People just naturally assume they will be fertile if they decide to start a family. . . . Because of its very nature, infertility is a private problem, because if the couple lets it be known that they are infertile, they receive a lot of gratuitous advice, like "just relax" or "have a second honeymoon." Well-intentioned friends all have names of a good doctor and stories of miracle babies. All of this fuels the gnawing desire to become pregnant, which in turn fuels the feeling of hopelessness.
>
> Then there is the anger; the anger at God, the anger at the doctors, but most of all the anger at one another. Feelings of guilt and unworthiness also play a part. . . . You begin to wonder if pregnancy is being withheld as a punishment from God.

Infertility serves as a painful reminder that there is a limit to man's resources. That's a tough lesson for us to learn. It was even more difficult in Rachel's day when a woman's self-worth was connected almost directly to the bearing of children—particularly sons. There was a sense of shame at not being able to fulfill God's command to "be fruitful and multiply."

Rachel was so frustrated that she arranged for her handmaid to represent her in the bedroom so she could get pregnant by her husband. (See Genesis 30:3-8.) Rachel was so jealous of Leah she was willing to take extreme measures. Surrogate parenting did not resolve Rachel's sense of frustration.

Sexual Problems. The competition between Rachel and Leah is almost embarrassing to read about today. It's no wonder there were problems in Jacob's marriage when he was not being sexually faithful to one mate. Rachel and Leah literally bartered for bedroom rights:

> During the wheat harvest, Reuben went out into the fields and found some mandrake plants, which he brought to his mother Leah. Rachel said to Leah, "Please give me some of your son's mandrakes" [The mandrake was a yellow fruit that some ancients believed would stimulate sensual desire and aid conception.]
>
> But she said to her, "Wasn't it enough that you took away my husband? Will you take my son's mandrakes too?"
>
> "Very well," Rachel said, "he can sleep with you tonight in return for your son's mandrakes" (Genesis 30:14, 15).

Rachel apparently thought the mandrakes would improve her sexual drive and possibly help her overcome her infertility. She compromised the intimacy of her relationship with Jacob in an attempt to heighten its physical rewards. Leah, on the other hand, found this another opportunity to attempt to please her husband sexually in her continuing effort to secure his love.

Rick Warren suggests that a man's sexual drive is like a light switch. It can be turned off and on quite quickly. But a woman's sexual drive is more like an iron—it takes time to warm up. It's like comparing a microwave with a crock-pot! Someone else has generalized, "A man will show love to get sex, while a woman will give sex to feel loved." When there is a major difference like that, there is potential for frequent conflict. Communication, patience, and unselfishness are essential for meaningful sex relations in marriage. Those qualities are hard enough to maintain in a monogamous relationship. Having multiple sex partners, whether by bigamy (like Jacob) or by affairs (like so many today), destroys the potential for a harmonious relationship.

There are dozens of potential conflicts in marriage. They may involve attitudes toward disciplining children, neatness, being on time, grammar, or just nagging habits that constantly irritate. There are big conflicts and small ones. Jacob and Rachel experienced some of the major ones.

Responses to Conflict

Since nearly every couple has conflict, the important issue is, "How do we respond when differences begin to surface in marriage?" Learning to confront conflict properly is one of the most important keys to a lasting and loving relationship.

Some respond by *explosion*. They rant, rave, throw things, curse—and even hit their spouses. Others respond with *tears*. Emotional temperaments burst into tears and often impede communication. Tears can be healthy at times, but they can also be a source of manipulation. Another response is *silence*. One wife complained that her husband, a linguist, could be silent in seven languages at the same time!

This is a favorite weapon of Christian people who know they are supposed to be mature. They know they're not supposed to get angry and explode, and they don't want to appear childish and weep, so they pout. They punish with silence.

"Is there something wrong?"

"No."

"Are you sure?"

"Yes."

"Do you want to talk?"

"No."

They aren't saying angry things, but they are making their mates suffer through chilling silence and prolonged alienation.

Silence is a very dangerous weapon. It eliminates communication while the hostility festers inside. We're never sure when we've been silent long enough to administer "justice."

The key to resolving conflict is that often talked about but seldom practiced art—communication. Ann Landers wrote,

The most important single ingredient in a marriage is the ability to communicate. If my mail is a fair reflection of what goes on with Mr. and Mrs. America behind closed doors, and I think it is, then most marriage problems stem from the inability of two people to talk to each other. How precious is the ability to communicate.... The man and wife who can air their differences, get the hostility out of their system and then kiss and make up have an excellent chance of growing old together.

Jacob and Rachel did not communicate well. She should have known Jacob's love for her wasn't dependant on the number of children she had. Somehow he had never convinced her of that.

The Resolution of Conflict

The Bible is still the best guide for effective communication. The more I read Scripture and observe life, the more impressed I am that the greatest wisdom in the world is found in God's Word. We can read the latest psychology and counseling manuals, but there is no advice more practical than what is found in the pages of the Bible. In learning how to resolve conflict, let's examine Ephesians 4:25-32. Here is a masterpiece of how to handle interpersonal relationships. Note four keywords when dealing with conflicts in a Christian marriage.

The first is *honesty*. Look at Ephesians 4:25: "Therefore each of you must put off falsehood and speak truthfully to his neighbor, for we are all members of one body." A harmonious relationship must be built on truthfulness. Nothing undermines trust more than deception. Honesty goes beyond just not lying; it includes telling your partner the truth about what you think and feel.

David Augsburger, in his book *Caring Enough to Confront*, captures the spirit of good communication, "I love you and since I love you I must tell the truth. I want your love. I also want your truth. Please love me enough to tell the truth."

You may have been taught to repress the truth to please people. Perhaps you've been conditioned not to hurt anyone's feelings— ever. You may be easygoing and pleasant to live with, but there is a danger that, while you are suppressing your real feelings, you are "stockpiling" resentment. You may temporarily avoid hurting your partner's feelings but ultimately undermine the relationship.

I counseled with a devastated Christian man who said, "I can't believe it! My wife just dropped a bombshell on me and said she wanted a divorce. She says the marriage is over; she has no feelings for me anymore. But honestly, I didn't even know we were in serious trouble. I thought we had a normal marriage!"

His wife responded, "I tried to tell him several times that I wasn't happy, but I didn't want to hurt his feelings, and he wouldn't listen to me."

Obviously, the husband was not very perceptive to his wife's feelings. But since she was dissatisfied over a long period of time, she had an obligation to express her true feelings more clearly. She had sugar-coated it so much that the urgent need didn't come through. Augsburger says,

> Avoiding honest statements of real feelings and viewpoints is often considered kindness, thoughtfulness or generosity. More often it is the most cruel thing I can do to others. It is a kind of benevolent lying. We often use selective honesty to protect ourselves or others.[5]

If you can't muster up the courage to confront your partner personally, then write it down. Communicate your concerns on paper. On the other hand, if you have a partner who is expressing discontent—listen! Don't fly off the handle. Don't ignore it. Pay attention. It's a good day in your marriage when you can be open enough to tell the truth and mature enough not to over-react. "Therefore put off falsehood and speak truthfully to your mate."

Honesty has some qualifiers. We're not supposed to be brutal or cruel. That suggests the second key word: *timing*.

Conflicts need to be confronted at an appropriate time. "In your anger do not sin. Do not let the sun go down while you are still angry, and do not give the devil a foothold" (Ephesians 4:26).

---

[5]David Augsburger, *Caring Enough to Confront* (Scottdale, PA: Herald Press, 1980), p. 25.

Notice the balance suggested in that verse. Don't sin in your anger. Don't approach your partner too quickly and explode. But don't suppress it for a lengthy time either. "Do not let the sun go down while you are still angry." Sometimes you can hold your tongue and the wrath goes away. You just forget it. Sometimes you restrain your anger and it festers inside and increases in intensity. If you don't confront it, you probably will blow the matter all out of proportion. It begins to poison your attitude toward everything in the relationship.

If, after waiting (and praying about it), the problem still irritates you, then it needs to be confronted at the proper time. Perhaps you need to wait until your mate is fed, the children are in bed, and the phone stops ringing. Then confront in love. We should develop such a perception about our mates that we know when they are the most receptive to a sensitive discussion.

If your partner is inclined to suppress irritations, you can assist by being alert to warning signs. Just as dogs growl before they bite, most people send out tell-tale signals when they're upset.

"When my husband gets real quiet and doesn't look me in the eye, I know something's wrong," said one wife.

"When she talks real fast to me on the phone and hangs up without saying goodbye, I know we need to spend some time talking," said a husband.

Maybe the warning sign is when he clears his throat or is continuously late. Maybe it's when she bites her nails or becomes hypercritical over little things. When you see those red flags, look for the appropriate time and say, "Honey, I sense something is wrong, and you're too important for me to let it slide. Will you tell me what it is?"

Deal with the problems as they arise. Find the appropriate time and the right setting. "Don't let the sun go down while you are still angry."

The third key word is *sensitivity*: "Do not let any unwholesome talk come out of your mouths, but only what is helpful for building others up according to their needs, that it may benefit those who listen" (Ephesians 4:29). All sorts of "unwholesome talk" can come out in the midst of conflict. Harsh criticism comes out. We know the verbal shots that can wound. We can be brutal in an attempt to get even.

Uncharacteristic profanity spews out. We get angry and curse at our partners; then we blame them for bringing out the worst in us.

Hateful threats come out. We warn, "I'm going to tell others what you're really like!"

"I'm going to leave!"

"I'll kill you!" might even erupt unexpectedly from our mouths.

Nasty sarcasm comes out, too. We use cutting remarks, gross exaggeration—anything that will wound and tear down. Proverbs 18:14 says, "A man's spirit sustains him in sickness, but a crushed spirit who can bear?"

Paul suggests that good communication guards against speech that tears down. Focus on speech that builds up. Choose your words carefully and guard your tone. Don't use inflammatory language. Don't be harsh. Don't shout or use a shrill voice. When you start shouting, that's evidence that you're out of control and the argument is weak. An ancient proverb says, "He who truly knows has no occasion to shout."

The tone of your speech may be more important than what you say. I can say the meanest things to my dog, and he wags his tail and wants to lick me—if I just say them in a nice tone. If I say kindly, "You're about the ugliest dog I've ever seen; yes you are!" He just wags his tail with joy. The opposite is true, too. I can shout and yell sweet nothings and he'll put his tail between his legs, get defensive, and growl at me.

Human beings are smarter than animals. But a sweet tone can disarm some of the most lethal disagreements. You can say so much more when you say it softly. The more shrill your tone, the less effective the communication. "A gentle answer turns away wrath, but a harsh word stirs up anger" (Proverbs 15:1).

The final key is *forgiveness*. "Get rid of all bitterness, rage and anger, brawling and slander, along with every form of malice. Be kind and compassionate to one another, forgiving each other, just as in Christ God forgave you" (Ephesians 4:31, 32).

One of the toughest assignments in marriage is to put the past behind you and go on. People say, "But you don't understand how I've been hurt. I'm justified in my resentment." Or, "He hasn't paid for it. I've got a right to hurt him back for what he did to me." Or, "I can't help it. I just can't forget it. I can't forgive her for what she did. I can't change the way I feel." Another might say, "My partner hasn't ever really asked for my forgiveness. Shouldn't he be begging me to give him another chance?"

People nurse grudges and wallow in self-pity. But bitterness barricades communication. One man said, "Every time my wife and I get into a conflict, she gets historical."

"You mean hysterical?" someone asked.

"No, historical," he said. "She brings up everything wrong I've ever done!"

The Bible says love "keeps no record of wrongs" (1 Corinthians 13:5). When you keep a record of wrongs, your partner is likely to go into a shell and refuse to discuss disagreements, concluding it's not worth the hassle. If you cannot forgive, you are enslaved by your feelings of bitterness and resentment. You are a prisoner of events that happened in the past that no one can change.

Your marriage cannot afford the luxury of self-pity or anger. You may be justified in your hurt; you may not have evidence of total remorse on the part of your partner. But is your pride worth losing your marriage or eliminating all possibility of companionship? We are instructed to "get rid of *all* bitterness." Put malice behind you. All you have is today. You can't change the past. You can't change your married partner. All you can change is you.

People ask, "How can I forgive? I just can't get it off my mind. It grates on me so much!" First, *make up your mind to forgive*. It's a matter of the will. Use your freedom to say, "I want to forgive that incident and go on because God has commanded me to do so." It's not an option.

Second, *behave in the proper manner*. "Be kind and compassionate," Paul says in Ephesians 4:32. He's talking about behavior, not feelings. Feelings change as behavior changes. As you express kindness to your partner, rather than resentment, your feelings change. It takes time, but they do change.

Then, *trust God to do His part*. He will renew your mind and transform your attitude. I know a wife whose husband ran away with another woman and was gone for over a year. Then he returned and asked for forgiveness. He wasn't very expressive, and she was angry, hurt, and insecure. But she was also determined to restore her marriage. With the help of God, after their initial discussion, she never brought the subject up again. During the next ten years, her husband got involved in a vibrant church and rededicated his life to the Lord and to his family. They have lived the last ten years of their life in harmony and companionship.

I've seen that kind of forgiveness take place on a number of occasions. I've also seen the reverse—when there is a stubborn refusal to forgive, the root of bitterness grows and consumes.

Adultery is not the only offense that inflicts deep wounds—there are dozens of others. Yet, whatever the offense, the one who clings to the misery of an unforgiving spirit will be crippled for life. The venom of hatred inflicts more damage to the vessel in which it is contained than the victim for whom it is intended.

I've never known anyone who forgave and then later regretted having done so. God is not asking you to do something impossible. "Forgive as the Lord forgave you" (Colossians 3:13). If anyone had a right to be bitter, it was Jesus. He was rejected, falsely accused, taunted, abused, tortured, lied about, and nailed to a cross. Yet He prayed, "Father, forgive them for they know not what they do." He set an example of forgiveness for us to follow.

If you choose to forgive, in time God will give you the grace to feel differently. Dr. Ed Wheat wrote,

As soon as you choose to forgive with your mind and your will, and commit the matter to God, you free both yourself and the one who offended you from the power of the past. Then whatever happened is historical fact and no longer emotional fact. In a real way you have opened up the wound to The Great Physician, and you will find that His love poured on it will so heal that you will no longer feel the sting.[6]

[6]Ed Wheat, *Love Life* (Grand Rapids: Zondervan, 1980), pp. 198, 199.

Let me add in closing, if you have a partner who is big enough to forgive, be humble enough to repent and grateful enough to express appreciation. That means much more than saying, "I'm sorry." It means ceasing whatever behavior caused the estrangement and giving no grounds for suspicion in the future. It means making a commitment to loving your partner the rest of your life.

Years ago, I heard that there are twelve words that keep a marriage relationship together. They are, "I was wrong; I am sorry; please forgive me; I love you." Those words need to be expressed frequently in your marriage if you are going to cope with conflicts constructively.

5

REAR GODLY CHILDREN

(AMRAM AND JOCHEBED)

Which of these two statements is true?

"Children are a great blessing to a marriage."
"Children put a great deal of pressure on a marriage."

Of course, both are true. Children are a tremendous blessing to a home. One of the greatest thrills that Judy and I have realized has been the privilege of rearing two boys. They enhance our marriage. They give us a source of conversation. They provide laughter and depth.

On the other hand, children can put tremendous pressure on a marriage, too. From the time the mother begins to expect a child and her appearance changes, there is pressure. When the baby cries all night with colic, and one of the parents has to sit up with her, and the other complains about the lack of sleep, there is pressure. When a baby needs changed and you have changed him ten times in a row, there is pressure. When the stroller won't fit in the trunk and it's ten degrees below zero and your mate asks what is wrong, there is pressure. When there is not much energy left for affection, when the mother disciplines and the dad doesn't understand how she can be so cruel, when the cost of schooling erodes the family budget, you discover the rearing of children produces a great deal of tension in the marriage.

A father came home and found his little boy sitting on the porch with his head in his hands and a forlorn expression on his face, and the father asked him what was wrong. The boy sat in silence for a little bit, and then confessed, "Just between you and me, Dad, I can't get along with your wife, either."

Having children can be a divisive factor in marriage. The number one problem in a second marriage has to do with children. The new spouse often feels he is playing second fiddle to his mate's children from the previous marriage. Or the natural parent becomes resentful of the interference on the part of the stepparent.

If a marriage is going to be what God wants it to be, it's important that both parents agree on a philosophy of child rearing.

There is a couple in the Bible whom I would consider to be among the most successful parents in history. Their strange names are Amram, the father, and Jochebed, the mother. The primary assignment of God's people is to rear godly children. That they fulfilled that assignment is seen dramatically in the life of their son Moses, who became one of the most impressive godly leaders in all of the Bible—in spite of the fact that he was reared against incredible spiritual odds.

But Jochebed and Amram were successful not only in the rearing of Moses, but their other two children were godly as well. Miriam, Moses' sister, was very actively involved in the celebration after the Israelites crossed the Red Sea. Aaron, Moses' brother, was the first high priest in Israel.

When a couple rears three children to be spiritual giants, they must be doing something right. There must be something in their approach that deserves emulation. Hebrews 11:23 reads, "By faith Moses' parents hid him for three months after he was born, because they saw he was no ordinary child, and they were not afraid of the king's edict."

Notice that both parents were involved. They were in agreement in their approach to child rearing. Since we have more information about Jochebed, we will focus primarily on her. But I think we will find that much of her example is valid for both mothers and fathers. This study will reveal several characteristics about this couple that will help both our marriages and our children.

Be Perceptive About Your Child's Potential

First they were perceptive about the potential of their child. In Exodus 2:2 we read that Moses' mother "saw that he was a fine child." Not every parent will say that about his child—that he's a "fine child." It's difficult to be objective about your own flesh and blood. If you ever watch a parent coach or teach his own child, he will almost always go to one extreme or the other. He will either be doting over the child or hassling him all the time. It's hard to be objective about your own child. Jochebed was not like that. She was perceptive, and she saw that he was a fine child. That is not just a mother's bias; the view is repeated three times in Scripture. Moses became a great leader.

She had other children, but she noticed he was more alert. She would have loved him had he been a handicapped child, but his obvious potential made her even more determined to spare his life.

It is a wise parent who can be objective and perceptive about his own child. Is your child a sanguine temperament who likes to have fun and please people? Is she a choleric who takes charge? Is your child a melancholy temperament? He's a good organizer but a very sensitive spirit. Is she a phlegmatic who goes with the flow and needs to be taught the value of work?

Children are not created equally in their temperament, and it takes discernment on the part of the parent to know the difference. Are you perceptive about your child's goals? When your child is young, what does he talk about becoming? Are those goals realistic and in line with his abilities or her gifts? Do you know which goals to dismiss and which ones to encourage? Psalm 127:4 says, "Like arrows in the hands of a warrior are sons born in one's youth." It's fitting that children are compared to arrows, because an arrow has to be aimed at something.

Zig Ziglar, in his book *See You at the Top*, says you can train fleas to stay in an open jar. You can put fleas in a coffee jar, punch holes in the top so they have air, and they will jump up and down in the jar, initially hitting the lid with every jump. After a while, they learn to jump just high enough so they don't hit the lid. They want the experience of jumping, but they don't want the pain of hitting the top of the lid. Then you can take the lid off, and they will not jump out. Ziglar says many parents put a lid on their children's potential when they are young. When the child says, "I want to be a missionary"; "I want to be a doctor"; "I want to make a million dollars"; "I want to write a book"; "I want to be a comedian," many parents will carelessly give them pain with inadvertent comments like, "Be realistic"; "I don't think that is what you want to do"; "You are just daydreaming; you can't do that."

My teenage son will occasionally say, "Dad, I would like to be mayor of Louisville some day." My instinct is to say, "Phil, you're not even a Democrat. How are you going to do that?" But his mother will say, "That's a great idea, Phil," and will encourage him.

Many children do not reach the height that they could because the parents have squelch the idea when they were little. I wonder what Jochebed said when Moses dreamed as a little boy, "Mom, someday I'm going to get us out of slavery." I think she was perceptive about his potential.

Are you perceptive about your child's gifts? Benjamin West, the painter, says that when he was a little boy he was baby-sitting with his sister. While his mother was gone, he got out some paper and found a paint set, and he tried to paint a portrait of his sister. He got paint everywhere. He says his mother came home from the grocery store, and the whole place was in disarray. But instead of blowing her stack, she went over and picked up the painting and said, "Oh, Benjamin! It's Sally, isn't it?" and she kissed him. West said, "That kiss made me a painter." His mother encouraged him in the area of his giftedness.

Is your child artistic? Athletic? Academically inclined? Wise parents objectively evaluate the child's temperament, the child's passion, and the child's talents. They don't try to force the child in an area of the parent's interest. It may mean that they wind up going to a Spelling Bee, or they wind up going to a concert when they are interested in athletics. But the Bible says you train up a child in the way that he should go, and when he's old he won't depart from it. Of course, that may mean spiritually, but I wonder if it couldn't mean vocationally, too. Be perceptive about your child's gifts. Encourage him in that area, and when he gets older, he will be gratified in that particular vocation.

I called my mother shortly before preaching on this passage once. I said, "Mom, I'm going to be preaching this Sunday on that passage of Scripture that says Moses' mother saw that he was a fine child when he was a little boy."

I was hoping she would say, "Well, you know, when you were a little boy, I saw that you were a fine child." But she just said, "Yes—"

I said, "Well, when I was a little boy, did you ever encourage me to be a preacher? I don't remember you ever saying anything."

"Oh, yes!" she said. "I said that to you often when you were very little. You would memorize Scripture at church, and I often said, 'Boy, you would be a good preacher some day. Maybe you should think about being a preacher.'"

I said, "Well, Mom, I never remember you saying anything to me when I was a teenager about doing that."

"Oh, no!" she said. "That would be the wrong time."

That was a wise response. Teenagers so often want to do just the opposite of what their parents say that they ought to do. I said, "Well, Mom, a month before I graduated from high school, when I surprised everybody and said that I was going to become a preacher, did that make you happy?"

She said, "Oh, I was tickled to death!" My sister told me that she cried, and she said, "That is just an answer to prayer!"

I can't help but wonder how much from those early years—even beyond my ability to recall—words of encouragement were etched on my mind that affected my decision later. Maybe I am a preacher today because there was a perceptive mother who saw a little boy and said, "This little boy likes to tell other people what to do. We'll make him a preacher!"

Be Creative in Combatting the World's Influence

Moses' parents were not only perceptive; they were creative. They used their creativity to counter the pressures of the world. When they learned that Pharaoh planned to kill all the male

Hebrew babies, they became aggressively innovative. They hid Moses for three months.

How did they do that? No matter how good a child is, it's hard to keep one quiet. Did you ever take a baby to a funeral or a wedding and try to keep him quiet? Babies make noises! But somehow Moses' parents kept him in seclusion and undetected for three anxious months. When they realized that this couldn't continue, they devised an ingenious plan.

Jochebed made a tiny waterproof bassinet, covering it with tar on the outside and the inside. I am sure she tested it for its seaworthiness many times over. She fashioned it inside with soft pillows and rags. Meanwhile, she was carefully observing the bathing habits of the Pharaoh's daughter. She knew the normal spot and the normal day that the princess would come with her entourage to swim. I don't think that Moses' ark floated down the Nile River and just happened by when the Pharaoh's daughter came out to bathe. I think the child's mother had cleverly arranged this unusual encounter.

The next step was to post a lookout. She stationed the baby's sister behind some bushes to watch and to respond appropriately. They must have rehearsed this scene by the hour: "Now don't appear to be too anxious. Don't call the baby by name. Be spontaneous. Say to Pharaoh's daughter, 'Ma'am, would you like for me to go get a Hebrew nursemaid?' and then you come and get me as quickly as you can."

What an ingenious plan! You know that Moses' mother couldn't sleep the night before. Her heart must have pounded and the tears flowed. She may well have spent the whole night praying for her baby, biting her lip not to curse Pharaoh. The next day, she put her little baby in the bassinet and left it along the Nile. She was determined that her child would not die. He would stay alive. He would be used of God.

Parents, if your children are going to stay alive spiritually in this dangerous age, you have to be innovative and aggressive as a Christian. We are living in a time when it is very difficult to rear godly children. Futurologist Alvin Toffler has written a book called *The Third Wave*. He says, if we define the family in today's

world as a husband, wife, and two or more children, and ask
how many Americans still live in this type of family, the aston-
ishing answer is a mere seven percent. Ninety-three percent of
the American people do not fit what used to be the normal image
of the family: father, mother, and two or more children.

We are living in an era when the family is breaking down and
the flow of society is working against us. The adversary is overtly
trying to kidnap and destroy your children. The Bible says, "Be
self-controlled and alert. Your enemy the devil prowls around
like a roaring lion looking for someone to devour" (1 Peter 5:8). If
you sit passively by, he is going to devour *your children* with the
philosophy of this world and will spiritually kill them.

Since we are involved in this spiritual warfare, it is essential
that we be alert and creative in response. Somebody was
watching the *Oprah Winfrey* show the other day and reported
that her topic was, "Teaching Your Child About Sex." (They always select bland topics for the afternoon talk shows!) Permissive parents on the show related how they supported pre-marital
sexual relations on the part of their teenagers. They said, "Let's
be honest; we can't expect our teenagers to practice abstinence
today. They are going to have relations whether we like it or not.
We would rather our teenagers do it at our house rather than be
sneaking around, so we have devised a signal. If they are making
love to their date in their bedroom when we come home, we ask
them just to put a green tape on the doorknob so that we won't
interrupt them."

That program is on at 4:00 in the afternoon, when teen-agers
are coming home from school and are tuning in. What kind of
signal is sent out? "Cool parents cooperate. Legalistic parents es-
tablish rules." That is the signal. Why not just hand them a sack
of cocaine and say, "Everybody is going to do it, so you might as
well do it here at the house; we'll make it easier for you."

The truth is, the attack on Christian values is relentless. The
teens' peers are telling them that drugs and alcohol are cool. The
education system tells them homosexuality is an acceptable life-
style, the movies endorse promiscuity, and even some preachers
and seminary professors suggest that the Bible is unreliable.

Mom and Dad, if your children are going to survive this spiritual onslaught, you cannot be passive and think they are going to learn sound moral principles by osmosis. You have to be creative and involved.

I have mixed emotions about home schooling. But I admit I greatly admire the parents who are so concerned about the spiritual values of their children that they spend the kind of time and energy that home schooling requires. Many parents are becoming creative in providing alternatives to television. There are Christian videos and Christian activities that can reinforce Biblical values rather than undermine them. We have a children's library at our church, and every week there are nearly 400 items checked out—almost 400 books and videos and various other items checked out of our *children's* library every week! Why? Because there are parents who are doing everything they can to teach spiritual values to their children.

When the son of one of our elders was baptized several months ago, the mother of the boy became very creative. She invited everybody who was involved in his baptism—Christian leaders, and his friends and family members—over to the house on Sunday night for the boy's first Communion service with his family. She made it a big event. There were cards and congratulations. They read the Bible. The mother explained Christ's death on the cross and the meaning of the loaf and the cup. And then the boy who had just been baptized passed Communion to everybody in the room, and he got to partake his first time. He will remember that for the rest of his life because there was a diligent, creative mother who wanted to make that a special event.

Several of our deacons' families have an annual visit from ancient shepherds at Christmastime. On Christmas Eve, several families get together and, instead of Santa Claus coming, there is a knock at the door and an old shepherd dressed in first-century garb comes in and sits down with the wide-eyed children and tells them about a spectacular event that he witnessed 2,000 years ago.

Be aware: when you get creative, it's risky. Jochebed and Amram could have lost their lives. If you dare to instill spiritual values in your child in a creative way, there will be some who think that you are going to the extreme. But the stakes are too high not to take the chance. Your child's eternal life hangs in the balance.

Moses later wrote in Deuteronomy 6, "You parents, love the Lord your God with all your heart, and these commandments that I have taught you, impress them onto your children. Talk about them when you walk along the way, and when you sit down and when you get up and when you lie down." In other words, don't segment Christianity to Sunday morning only, parents. Talk about the Lord as naturally in your daily conversation as you talk about sports or dress or what is on television.

When my teenage son is struggling with an issue, his mother will often say, "Phil, I'm going for a walk; do you want to go along? Let's go see how the golf course is doing." They will walk for an hour or so, and the barriers will break down as they talk casually. Often he will come back with a completely different spirit and say, "You know, Dad, I have been thinking about this. I think it would be the Lord's will that thus and so transpire." Just talk about spiritual things naturally in everyday conversation, and you will impress them on your child. You must do that because your enemy, the devil, is a roaring lion seeking to destroy.

Be Responsive to Your Child's Changing Needs

There is one more trait in Moses' mother that parents today need to observe: she was mature in her reaction to her son's development. Jochebed's clever plan unfolded just as if she had written the script. Pharaoh's daughter came to bathe, found the bassinet, and fell in love with the baby. Miriam ran to get the mother. "Oh, Mother! He is going to be okay! Pharaoh's daughter found him and fell in love with him. It's going to be okay. She wants you."

Can't you see Jochebed wiping the tears, hurrying down to the riverbank trying to be casual? "What have we here? Oh, somebody has abandoned a baby. My, isn't that the cutest baby you have ever seen in your life?" Then, Exodus 2:9 says, "Pharaoh's daughter said to her, 'Take this baby and nurse him for me, and I

will pay you.'" Aren't God's ways incredible? He not only pre-
served Moses' life, but He arranged for Moses' mother, a slave, to
rear him and to get paid for it. The Bible says God "is able to do
immeasurably more than all we ask or imagine" (Ephesians 3:20).
This plan worked to perfection.

Jochebed spent the next few years nurturing and training
Moses. We don't know how long she had him. Some have specu-
lated it was as few as seven years; others say twelve years. But
she took advantage of every opportunity to impress on this child
who God was and what was expected of him. She was taking advantage of those formative years, and when the time came for
Jochebed to release Moses to Pharaoh, Moses had those Jewish
concepts of morality and monotheism etched deep into his soul
so he would never forget.

Actually, Jochebed went through the same process that every
mother and dad have to go through. It was just compressed into a
shorter period of time. All parents have to take advantage of the
time God gives them to instill proper values in their children.
Then they must release their children to live out those values.

Parents, be careful not to release your children too soon.
Sometimes parents grow weary and they think of themselves as
progressive and they give too much freedom. When grade-school
children can roam the neighborhood all summer long with no accountability, when junior-high students can go out to the malls at
night and roam around with no accountability, then somebody
has released them too early. When teenagers can sit in church
service and talk out loud during the service or go out in the
hallway and never come in, somebody has released them too
early. When seniors in high school can spend prom night in a
motel room, somebody is being too permissive! Young people
need to know where the parameters are. The rules provide security. The rules provide an appreciation of freedom when they are
relaxed. If there aren't any rules to be relaxed, however, then
there is no experience of freedom, and there is resentment and
rebellion on the part of the children later.

It's also difficult to release the child when that time comes. It's
hard to let go and watch your child go off to college—perhaps

hundreds of miles from home. It's tough when your child takes a job out of town and moves out to make a life and family of his own. So I would like to close this chapter by giving some tangible suggestions to make releasing your child more successful.

Number one, *make the marriage the center of your home* from the beginning. Make the *marriage* the center of your home—not the children. Children are a blessing to a marriage, but they are not the focal point of the home. Remember, Mom and Dad, you and your partner will be together long after your children are gone. Let the children know that they are important, but make it clear they are the second most important thing in your life. Go out on dates with your married partner. Get away from your children on occasion. Let them know your loyalty is to each other.

Some time ago, I preached almost an entire sermon on this very point. I said, "If you have a child-centered home, that teaches the child to be selfish. He thinks he is the center of the world, and it puts the marriage in jeopardy." Steve Chapman, a songwriter in Nashville, heard that message on tape and wrote a song entitled "Before There Was You." Look at the words of that song:

Children, please give me your kind attention.
I have something to say, here's my intentions.
I'm gonna go out with your mother tonight,
And no, you can't come; it won't help if you cry.

Oh, you may wonder how I could be
So heartless to want just your mother and me.
Well, she's your dear mother; I know that it's true.
But she was my sweetheart before there was you.

First we'll walk by the ocean, and we're gonna hold hands.
We'll write our names in the wet sand,
We'll write "I love you's"—send them off in a bottle,
Then in memory of you, we'll eat at McDonalds.

[My sermons don't elicit deep theology, but that's practical!]

And she's still my sweetheart even though there is you,
And she'll be my sweetheart when there's no more of you.[7]

Parents be realistic. You are going to spend about $100,000 per child, and when they get to be fifteen, they won't want to be seen with you in public! So there better be something more in your life than that. When you make the marriage a priority, it takes the pressure off the children to perform and please you all the time, and it gives them security.

Number two, *fill your child with the Word of God early.* David said, "I have hidden your word in my heart that I might not sin against you" (Psalm 119:11). The easiest time to memorize Scripture is when one is young. Jochebed had Moses for just those formative years, and she took advantage of it. That ought to be especially encouraging to single parents, whose time with their children is often limited. Take advantage of the formative years; then you can send them off with confidence.

Number three, *set down tangible benchmarks of freedom.* Releasing your child is not an abrupt event. It is a progressive experience from the time the child is born. Maybe the ages will vary according to your opinion, but you can say something like, "When you get to be twelve, if you are responsible, we'll consider letting you ride your bicycle to school. When you are fifteen, we will consider maybe allowing you a few double dates. When you are sixteen, if your grades are good, then maybe you can drive a car. When you are a sophomore in college, we'll consider allowing you to have your own car."

When young people have those definite dates to look forward to, it creates a sense of progress and maturity.

Number four, *let your children know when they are on their own and then treat them like adults.* I remember my mother's saying, when I went off to college, "We have done everything we can. Now you are on your own; you are an adult now." When I

---

[7]Steve and Annie Chapman, "Before There Was You," © 1990, Times and Seasons Music. Used by permission.

came home for the summer, I knew that there were certain guidelines that I better observe, but there were no more of those curfews, no more of those rules, and I responded accordingly.

Dr. James Dobson took a survey of over 2,000 married people and asked what was the number-one problem with parents. He expected them to say in-laws, but only eleven percent said that. By far, the number-one problem, cited by forty-four percent of the respondents, was the failure of the parents to let go after the children were married. The parents continued to interfere in finances and in child rearing and occupations and attempted to tell the children how to run their lives.

As a parent of adults, I can tell you it is hard not to manipulate, not to pout, not to threaten to cut them out of the will! But treat them like adults. Give advice only when you are asked—and then give it sparingly. Then they will appreciate you, and you will have a unique relationship with them as adults to adults. When you ask them, "Are you coming home this Christmas?" and they say "No, not this Christmas," just say, "Okay, hope you can come home next year." Don't say, "Okay, hope you can come home next year if I am still alive. This cold is really bad this year. I am fifty-five years old; you never know—" Don't do that. Don't manipulate them. Give them freedom.

Somebody said, "What you release you keep; what you hold onto you lose." There comes a time when you have to say, "I have done my best; now you are on your own." Then, when they come to visit you, you can at least rejoice in knowing that they are there because they want to be.

Finally, once you release them, *pray for them every day*. The Bible says the fervent prayer of a righteous man avails much. Moses' mother was probably disappointed in him at times. When he was forty, he lost his temper and murdered an Egyptian. He had to flee the country. But if Jochebed was still alive, years later when he came back to lead the Hebrew slaves out of bondage, she was the proudest woman in Israel. Don't give up on them. Keep praying every day.

It is said that Abraham Lincoln saw a very attractive young black woman at the slave block one day, and he began to bid on her. The bidding went higher and higher, but Lincoln finally bought her. She thought she was purchased to be used and abused and discarded. But as they walked away from the slave block, Abraham Lincoln said to her, "Now you are free."

She defiantly said, "What does that mean?"

He said, "That means you are free."

She said, "You mean, I am free to say whatever I want to say?"

He said, "Yes."

"I am free to do whatever I want to do?"

"Yes."

"I am free to go wherever I want to go?"

"Yes."

And she burst into tears and said, "I guess, then, I will go with you."

It's a great day, even though we paid this exorbitant price, to say to our children, "You are free," and to hear them say, "I think I will go where you go. I think I will follow your Lord. I think I will marry a Christian. I think I will teach my children just the way you taught me."

6

PRESERVE THE MARRIAGE

(DAVID AND BATHSHEBA)

King David was a great man. The Bible calls him a man after God's own heart. David was a humble shepherd who obediently served God as a boy in obscurity. He was a courageous youth who valiantly confronted the giant Goliath when no one else dared. He was a talented poet who wrote hymns that God's people still sing today. David was a loyal servant to King Saul, playing music to soothe the king's troubled spirit.

He then became a patient fugitive, refusing to take the king's life when he had a perfect opportunity—and, many would have said, a perfect right—to do so. He became a spiritual king who returned the ark of the covenant to Jerusalem and intended to build a magnificent temple. David was a compassionate leader who invited Saul's crippled grandson to live in the palace with him until he died.

David distinguished himself as a man of God, a composer of psalms, and a leader of men who just oozed with charisma. Even so, his record was not without blemish.

David had trouble at home, and eventually his marriage fell apart altogether. Look at 1 Kings 15:5: "For David had done what was right in the eyes of the Lord and had not failed to keep any of the Lord's commands all the days of his life—except in the case of Uriah, the Hittite." It is that exception that forms the focus of this chapter.

One night, when the king couldn't sleep, he took a stroll on the rooftop patio away from the crowded street where he could enjoy the out of doors. David was now at the peak of his career. Other kings were going off to battle. He delegated that responsibility and started to enjoy his success.

That night, as he leaned over the railing and looked out over the city, he saw a beautiful woman step out onto her patio next door, getting ready to bathe. The Bible says very frankly that Bathsheba was very beautiful. David's eyes were fixed. His heart began to pound as he watched. I wonder why Bathsheba didn't use partitions or pull the shades. Why did she deliberately bathe on the rooftop, knowing that the patio of the king was right next door? She was either very careless, or she was deliberately trying to attract his attention. David was enraptured by her beauty. Then he inquired as to her identity.

Up to this point, he had been so involved in his work that he didn't even know who lived next door. Now he asks who she is. Verse 3 of 2 Samuel 11 reads, "And David sent someone to find out about her. The man said, 'Isn't this Bathsheba, the daughter of Eliam and the wife of Uriah the Hittite?'" Now, that is a very unusual genealogy. Ordinarily, when the ancients discussed identity, they talked about the parents and the grandparents. Seldom was there a reference to a mate. But this servant knew his master. He knew what David was thinking, and he said, "David, she is the daughter of Eliam but the wife of Uriah, one of your military men. She is married, David."

Many times when you are tempted, God will send a warning of some kind. The counsel of a friend, the interruption of your plans, a phone call from a child, a song on the radio. There will often be some last-minute siren urging you to alter your course. But David had stared too long. In his lust, he forgot who he was, and he forgot how many people would be affected by his sin. All that mattered to him at that moment was the gratification of his appetite.

So David sent for Bathsheba, and she apparently came willingly, and they committed adultery.

The Bible says that there is pleasure in sin "for a season." No doubt, this act carried with it excitement, romance, and intrigue. David and Bathsheba probably rationalized that they were meant for each other; they were both lonely. But it was a prelude to disaster. That moment of pleasure was followed by an unwanted pregnancy and an attempt to cover up. Lies, deceit, drunkenness, the murder of Uriah, the death of the child! Chaos in David's family; disrespect in the nation.

David's story provides the basis for a discussion about marriages that break down. Throughout this book, we have been looking at God's plan for marriage and love in the home. But if marriage was ordained by God to be the highest of all human relationships, why do so many marriages fall apart? More importantly, what can we do to prevent that kind of disaster from occurring in our own homes?

Why Marriages Break Down

Let's first try to understand the problem. Why are marriage vows broken? I am convinced that David's home did not break down suddenly. A. W. Tozer once said, "No man suddenly goes base." I don't think that all was well with David spiritually and domestically one day, and the next day he fell over the cliff into adultery.

A study of the Scripture indicates to me that David had been on a spiritual and domestic drift for some time. Let's read some Scripture verses that trace the history of David's marriage to Michal, his first wife.

In 1 Samuel 18:20 and 21, we read, "Now Saul's daughter Michal was in love with David, and when they told Saul about it, he was pleased. 'I will give her to him,'" . . . he thought. This was an arranged marriage, but David had problems with his father-in-law from the very beginning. Saul was jealous of him and tried to kill him. In fact, the rest of verse 21 says Saul agreed to the marriage so that Michal would "be a snare" to David and get him killed! Instead, Michal helped David to escape her father (1 Samuel 19:11, 12).

In 1 Samuel 19:13, we read that Michal took an idol and laid it on the bed, covering it with a garment and putting some goat's hair on the head. To her credit, she helped David, her husband, escape, but she put an idol in the bed, covering it over to make it appear that he was still there. The question is, "What was she doing with an idol in the home?" David was a man after God's own heart, but apparently there was a spiritual disparity between him and his wife.

So there were in-law problems; there was a spiritual disparity; and then, when David ran away as a fugitive, Saul gave Michal to another man, and there was unfaithfulness. In the meantime, as a fugitive, David married another woman, Abigail. When David finally became king, he brought Michal back into the palace, but there were continual problems.

In the book of 2 Samuel, the sixth chapter, King David was leading the ark of the covenant back into Jerusalem and celebrating in the front of the parade. Verse 16 reads, "As the ark of the Lord was entering the City of David, Michal daughter of Saul watched from a window. And when she saw King David leaping and dancing before the Lord, she despised him in her heart." She had grown up with the sophistication of the palace. When she saw David celebrating so effusively in front of people, she was repulsed by it. Verse 20 reads, "When David returned home to bless his household, Michal daughter of Saul came out to meet him and said, 'How the king of Israel has distinguished himself today, disrobing in the sight of the slave girls of his servants as any vulgar fellow would!'"

Here was David at his moment of great glory, and instead of encouraging him, she was jealous of him or turned off by his behavior, and she discouraged him. Wrong reaction. Because the man's ego is so weak, it's hard to take that.

Years ago, I was playing on our church softball team, and we finished in fourth place in the nation in a tournament in Petersburg, Virginia. I had a good tournament. I made good catches, I hit pretty well, and I was diving into bases. Finally, after the last game, I walked over to where my wife was. I expected her to say, "Oh, you were great! I am so proud of you, my hero." What she said was, "Where are we going to eat?" Then she added, "Boy, that uniform is dirty; you better get it off before we drive."

It is only by my deep spiritual commitment that I did not file for divorce right there! Every man wants to be the hero. He wants to be encouraged by his wife. Yet Michal, at the moment of David's greatest glory, said, "Boy, did you make a fool out of yourself today, hotshot." And it ticked David off, too.

> David said to Michal, "It was before the Lord, who chose me rather than your father or anyone from his house when he appointed me ruler over the Lord's people Israel—I will celebrate before the Lord. I will become even more undignified than this, and I will be humiliated in my own eyes. But by these slave girls you spoke of, I will be held in honor" (2 Samuel 6:21, 22).

You see the kind of sarcasm and unkindness that is being exchanged there? "If you don't like it, there are some other women who do!"

The final verse of this section tells us from that time on, Michal had no children to the day of her death. This is a problem they could not control. But the disappointment of infertility contributed to their stress. David had been on a spiritual and domestic drift for some time, and then came the adultery with Bathsheba. Somebody said, "Marriages don't blow up; they fizzle out."

The important thing to notice here is God's reaction to David's sin. God did not say, "David, you have committed adultery with Bathsheba, but I understand. You have had a lot of problems with Michal, she has not encouraged you, and you have had in-law problems; there has been infertility, and you are really frustrated—it's understandable." No. God sent Nathan the prophet to David, and Nathan said, "You have stolen your neighbor's wife, you have despised the Word of the Lord, and you have committed that which is evil in God's eyes."

God considers adultery the ultimate offense to a marriage. I hear people rationalize, "Well, he had an affair, but you can hardly blame him the way his wife gained weight." Or, "She had an affair, but you can hardly blame her the way he was out of town all the time." But God makes no such allowances.

When people get married, they make a promise to each other and to God to be faithful, for better or for worse, and to give

themselves to each other and to each other *only* as long as they
both shall live. When an affair occurs, it occurs because somebody has decided to put his own selfish desires ahead of God's
will and ahead of the well-being of his mate. That is the reason
Hebrews 13:4 says, "Marriage should be honored by all, and the
marriage bed kept pure, for God will judge the adulterer and all
the sexually immoral." The union between husband and wife is
sacred, and it is exclusive in God's sight. That is the reason Jesus
said, "Anyone who divorces his wife, except for marital unfaithfulness, and marries another woman commits adultery"
(Matthew 19:9). Marital unfaithfulness was the one sin that Jesus
singled out as severing the marriage vow.

I understand the Scripture to teach that you are married when
you comply with the legal requirements of society and your relationship is physically consummated. When you and your partner
disagree over finances or Sunday school class or child rearing,
you are still in the will of God. But when you unite with somebody else physically, you have broken that promise to your mate,
and you are doing that which to God is a serious breach of integrity.

Look at 1 Corinthians 6:16. "Do you not know that he who
unites himself with a prostitute is one with her in body? For it is
said, 'The two will become one flesh.'" So, "Flee from sexual im-
morality. All other sins a man commits are outside his body," the
Bible says, "but he who sins sexually sins against his own body"
(1 Corinthians 6:18). There are a number of sins that are destruc-
tive to a marriage. But sexual sin is particularly damaging. It
severs that sacred union.

I know of a wife who discovered that her husband had been
unfaithful to her in kind of a one-night stand on a business trip,
and she was crushed. She sobbed and she sobbed, and her husband tried to comfort her by saying, "Honey, I'm sorry. But it really didn't mean anything to me, and you are making a bigger
deal out of it than it really is." That was no comfort. To her, that
union was sacred. To *God* it was sacred. When we begin trying to
treat the sexual union as unimportant, it's an indication that we
don't have a sensitivity for the sacredness of marriage.

Why Marriages Do Not Break Down

The important thing is that we learn to exercise prevention. The book of Jude closes with a doxology addressed, "To him who is able to keep you from falling" (Jude 24). God *is* able to keep you from falling. He is able to keep you in harmony with your marriage vows. So there ought to be some things that the Christian can do because of his commitment to Christ that makes the marriage affair proof.

Here are five things I think we can do. First, *be fearful of the consequences.* Fear can be a healthy deterrent to sin. We try to keep our young people off drugs by using fear as a legitimate motive. We say, "Look, drugs can kill you, drugs are illegal, and they can fry your brain, and you can wind up in jail." We know fear can be a deterrent to sin.

The Bible says the wages of sin is death. Sin can look so good in prospect, but it is so devastating in retrospect. Remember the pain of the harvest always exceeds the pleasure of the sowing. One constant prevention for an affair is to understand where that road will take you. The Bible says, "Be sure your sin will find you out." Once you start down that slippery slope, you are skidding toward unbelievable emotional pain. Are you really willing to pay the price financially, emotionally, and spiritually? Have you considered disappointing your children, contracting a disease, threatening your career, and living outside the will of God? Even if your spiritual commitment is weak, be smart enough to stay off that road. Some people say, "Well, you know, the worst that can happen is I could end up in divorce, and that wouldn't be so bad because my marriage is not great anyway."

Diane Medved, in her book *The Case Against Divorce,* wrote, "Unfortunately people who have an unrealistic view of marriage usually have an unrealistic view of divorce. When you are in the grip of a marital crisis, it's easy to overlook the fact that the typical divorced person spends six months to two years in a zombie-like state traumatized by the event."[8] She adds, "Remember this,

[8]Diane Medved, *The Case Against Divorce* (New York: D. I. Fine, 1989).

too, it's not easy to find someone else who understands your quirks, who wants the same things out of life, and who shares your past experiences and connections." Almost every divorced person I talk to says, "Bob, when you are talking to people, tell them that divorce is horrible, that it is not easy, that the consequences are beyond the imagination, and it's not over when the divorce papers are served up. And it's no fun to play the dating game again. The pickings are not as good as I imagined," they say.

Walter Davis, age thirty-three, divorced his wife Barbara. A few months later, he applied to a computer dating service. He filled out an exhaustive questionnaire and paid a healthy fee. Out of 30,000 prospects, the computer kicked out only four names of people who would be compatible with him, and the first name on the list was his former wife, Barbara!

Understand the consequences. Be smart. Be faithful to your mate, even though he's not perfect, because the road to an affair ends in disaster.

Second, *be aware of your vulnerability*. Nobody is exempt. The Bible says, "Take heed when you think you stand, lest you fall." David was a man after God's own heart. But he still had problems. You may have been married for twenty-five years. You may have a good record. You may go to church. But you need to be aware of your vulnerability.

Drs. Minirth and Meier suggest that over forty percent of American husbands are unfaithful to their wives. Forty percent! But, they add, as our income increases, so does the likelihood of having an affair. They state that if your income is over $70,000 a year, the chances of an affair increase to seventy percent. They suggest three reasons for that. One, power; two, the habit of acquisition; and three, the reward mentality: "I have earned it; I want a trophy for a wife."

It was in David's success that the temptation came. He was familiar with power. He knew how to get things done his way.

I would recommend a book for you. It's entitled *Hedges*, by Jerry Jenkins. He wrote, "One of the major causes of marital breakups in the Christian community is the lack of protective hedges that the spouse should plant around their marriage.

Because of the new openness in society to interaction between the sexes, I have placed the following hedges around my marriage," he says.

Number one, whenever I need to meet or dine or travel with an unrelated woman I make it a threesome. Should an unavoidable last minute complication make this impossible, my wife hears it from me first.

Number two, I am careful about touching. While I might shake hands or squeeze an arm or a shoulder in greeting, I embrace only dear friends or relatives, and only in front of others.

Number three if I pay a compliment it is on clothing or hair style, not on the person herself. Commenting on a pretty outfit is much different in my opinion than telling her that she herself looks really pretty.

Four, I avoid flirtation or suggestive conversation even in jest.

Number five, I remind my wife often in writing and orally that I remember my wedding vows.[9]

You may think that is restrictive, but I think those hedges help to prevent a failure.

Third, *be alert to the warning signs.* Most marriages don't blow up, they fizzle out. Be alert to the danger signs. Be alert to the fact that the light may be flickering. The decline may begin with an increased desire for individual activity: "I want my space." There may be frequent bickering over nonsense; things that didn't matter before become big deals. Perhaps there is a sense of distancing in the marriage, or a declining interest in sexual activity that has nothing to do with getting older or being tired. That may be accompanied by an increase in secrets and deception. Interest in the things of God and the church declines, replaced by an increased interest in the things of the world and Satan. There is lying and a refusal to be accountable. "I don't ask you where you are every hour of the day; just leave me alone."

[9]Jerry Jenkins, *Hedges* (Brentwood, TN: Wolgemuth and Hyatt, 1989).

Wayne Smith told me about a developer in Fayette County, Kentucky, who came in at six in the morning, and his wife asked him, "Where have you been?"

He said, "Well, I got in kind of late, and I sat on the porch swing and I went to sleep on the porch swing, and I spent the night there."

She said, "The porch swing? I took that down a month ago!"

He said, "That is my story and I am sticking to it."

Unbelievable—the lies and the lack of accountability.

Another warning sign is a radical change in appearance. I think husbands and wives need to watch their weight and guard their appearance for one another. But beware when there is a sudden change in appearance. He perms his hair and goes to the fitness center to lift weights, and he starts wearing red bikini briefs instead of boxer shorts—that is a time to be suspicious! Then there are rumors about unfaithfulness, followed by denial. Be alert to those danger signs in a marriage. If you see them happening in yourself, repent and break it off completely. Learn to hang up the phone. Learn to say no to the invitation for a lunch. Even change a job, if necessary. It is not worth the price that you are going to pay!

If you see those danger signs in your mate, and he stubbornly refuses to acknowledge them, I would suggest you read Dr. James Dobson's book, *Love Must Be Tough*, and act accordingly.

The fourth thing we can do to prevent an affair is to *be creative in marriage*. Marriage can get into a rut that becomes too predictable. Occasionally, we need to do something that alters the routine. Eat someplace different. Take a trip to someplace you have not been. Do the unexpected, like listen to her when she talks. Or spend less money than he anticipates. Or give a gift of flowers. Or be more aggressive sexually.

Wives, throw away that nightgown that you have worn since 1981 and get something different. Husbands, learn to be verbal and romantic in your expression to your wife. Did you hear about the letter that Sullivan Ballou wrote to his wife just before he died? Ballou was a thirty-two-year-old Providence lawyer and former speaker of the Rhode Island House of Representatives, and he left his career to volunteer for the Union army in the Civil War. One week before he fell mortally wounded in the first battle of Bull Run, he wrote this poignant letter to his wife Sarah.

It is [my] prayer . . . that I shall return to my loved ones unharmed. If I do not my dear Sarah never forget how much I loved you nor that when my last breath escapes me on the battle field it will whisper your name.

Forgive my many faults and the many pains I have caused you. How thoughtless, foolish I have oftentimes been! How gladly would I wash out with my tears every little spot upon your happiness and strugle [sic] with all the misfortunes of this world to shield you and my children from harm, but I cannot. I must watch you from the spirit world and hover near you while you buffet the storms with your precious little freight. . . .

But, oh Sarah! if the dead can come back to this earth and flit unseen around those they love I shall be always with you in the brightest day and the darkest night amidst your happiest sceans [sic] and gloomiest hours. Always, always. And when the soft breeze fans your cheek, it shall be my breath; or the cool air your throbbing temple, it shall be my spirit passing by. Sarah, do not mourn me dead. Think I am gone and wait for me for we shall meet again.[10]

All the men reading this book are saying about now, "That is the corniest thing I have ever heard in my life!" The women are saying, "Oh, that is lovely. I wish my husband had been in the Civil War!"

I didn't know whether to read that in a sermon or not, so I read it to a preacher friend of mine, and he said, "No, that is too mushy." I read it to my wife and said, "What do you think?" I looked up, and tears were streaming down her face.

The men are thinking, "Yeah, wives, you dress up and look more provocative when we are going to bed." And the woman

[10]*Sullivan Ballou Letter, July 14, 1861.* From the Adin Ballou Papers, Illinois State Historical Library, Springfield, Illinois.

says, "That makes me so uncomfortable." The women are thinking, "Yeah, men, you be more romantic; be more exciting; you express your love like that." And the men are saying, "Oh, that is so uncomfortable; that is so corny." Learn to be creative. Give of yourself to your mate to make your marriage more exciting.

Finally, and most importantly, *be content with the ordinary*. Just be content with the ordinary! One of the primary problems of marriage is unrealistic expectations. We enter marriage thinking it's going to be romance and security, and it winds up being uncertainty and routine. We enter marriage thinking that sex is going to be like thunder over the Ohio, and it winds up being more like a sparkler over Beargrass Creek, and we are disappointed. There is disillusionment.

Well, pizzazz has its place in marriage, but so does endurance. Marriage is companionship, it's routine, it's dependability, it's faithfulness to one another. When a person loses his mate, he hardly ever talks about the trip to the Bahamas. What he misses are those ordinary things. He will say, "You know, after church on Sunday night, she used to grab my arm when we walked to the car and say, 'Boy it's been a good day.' I just miss her so much on Sunday night." Or, "You know, when University of Kentucky played basketball on TV, he would sit in that chair, and he would yell at the referee, and every time UK comes on TV, I just really miss hearing him yell." Little things.

Paul told the Philippian Christians, "I have learned the secret of being content in any and every situation because I can do all things through Christ who strengthens me." When Christ is really the center of our lives, we learn to be content with the little blessings of life. When self is at the center, we are always comparing, always wondering, always restless. But one of the marks of spiritual maturity is the ability to appreciate the ordinary. The ability to say with the psalmist, "This is the day the Lord has made; let us rejoice and be glad in it" (Psalm 118:29).

In closing I want to say a word to those of you who have already experienced some of the consequences of an affair. You might right now be living in the wake of the problem. If your marriage has been shattered by *your* sin, then you seek forgiveness. David was guilty of adultery. He confessed that sin and he received God's forgiveness. The Bible assures us that David is in Heaven today. The grace of God is unbelievable, and it's available to you today. You can't go back and relive the past, but you can pick up where you are right now and, by God's grace, erase your sin from the record—if you will truly repent. First John 1:9 says, "If we confess our sins, he is faithful and just and will forgive us our sins and purify us from all unrighteousness." So why don't you humbly say with David in Psalm 51: "Wash away all my inequity . . . and I will be clean; wash me, and I will be whiter than snow"?

To those who have been the victim of an unfaithful partner, if your marriage has been devastated by grief, then seek restoration. There are some marriages that can't be restored, and you have to pick up where you are and live a life of integrity and just go on. But if you have been the victim of an affair and it's still possible to keep it together, don't throw away your marriage because of your crushed pride or your vindictive spirit. It's asking a lot for you to forgive and start trusting again, but it's possible. There are thousands of people who have done it before you. And with the help of God, you can do it too.

Jesus said, "With God, all things are possible." Paul said, "I can do all things through Christ who strengthens me."

Swallow your pride. Get it together. Forgive—even as the Lord has forgiven you!

7

START OVER

(BOAZ AND RUTH)

Years ago, when my two-year-old car needed a new battery, one of my sons would say, "Dad, we need to buy a new car. This one is getting old." When I had a little trouble with the tape deck, they would say, "Dad, we need a new car. This one is eating us out of house and home." I kept insisting that there was no reason to spend thousands of dollars on a new car just because our familiar one needed minor repairs.

Marriages are a little bit like that. One of the purposes of this book has been to encourage couples to stay with their relationships. Sometimes just a little bit of maintenance can get the marriage operating smoothly again. Occasionally, there is a serious breakdown, and a complete overhaul is necessary. But most problems are resolvable. Even if there has been an affair, that doesn't mean the marriage can't be repaired if we pay the price of repentance and forgiveness.

One of the problems of our society has been the tendency of so many couples to give up too quickly on their marriages. As soon as there is a minor problem, they begin to look admiringly at other models. They soon convince themselves that nothing can be done, the old relationship is over and headed for the junk pile. Before long, however, they discover that the trade-in is costly and that they have merely bought into a whole new set of problems.

So I trust that I have made God's Word clear. God intends for a husband and a wife to be committed to one another in love till death do them part. But what do you do if the marriage relationship really is over?

When I was in college, I owned a '57 Nash Rambler. It was about six years old, and it was falling apart. A mechanic told me that it was beyond repair, and he urged me to get rid of it before it killed me. So I tried to trade it in on a '60 Ford. The used car dealer that tried to sell me the Ford said, "If you buy this for cash, I will sell it to you for $1100. If you trade in the Rambler, it will be $1200." I had to admit that the days of the Rambler were over.

What do you do if a marriage is over? Maybe your spouse has walked out on you and gone off with somebody else, or you concluded years ago that your marriage was irreparable and you gave up on it, and it cannot be reclaimed. Or perhaps your mate has died and you live alone. Is it Scriptural for you to start over with somebody else? Is it possible for you to remain single the rest of your life and be fulfilled and happy?

The story of Boaz and Ruth is a model for starting over. This is a very pertinent story because it focuses on single people. Did you know it is now estimated that, by the year 2000, fifty-one percent of our adult population will be single? That makes this a pertinent story because the main characters in the story are single people.

It's No Sin to Be Single

There is Naomi, who is an older Jewish widow. Her husband had moved from Bethlehem of Judah to the country of the Moabites. There they had two sons. Their sons grew up and married Moabite women, but then tragedy struck. Naomi's husband died, and oddly enough her two sons died about the same time. So here is a woman living with grief and struggling against bitterness toward God.

The second main character is Ruth. She is the daughter-in-law of Naomi, and now she is a young widow with no children. She had relatives in Moab, but apparently she was closer to Naomi, her mother-in-law, than to anybody else. Ruth was grieving; she was lonely; she was uncertain about what to do with her life.

In the middle of the story, a single man, a middle-aged man by the name of Boaz, steps on stage. Boaz is a wealthy Jewish landowner, much older than Ruth, but he is about to become her second husband. Apparently Boaz has never married; he must have been single all his life.

I checked our church files to see how many single people we have on our membership roll. We have close to 1500 single people age 22 and up. We minister to a lot of singles! Nor is our church unusual. It's made up of people just like you and the people you know. So what's true about our church is probably very similar to what you would find if you did a survey of the people around you. That makes this a very relevant story.

Our singles can be divided into three very distinct categories. There are those who, like Naomi and Ruth, have lost their mates to death. That is one of the most difficult adjustments in life. The Bible says that, when people get married, the two become one. So there is a sense in which, when your mate dies, you feel incomplete and out of place.

I have read that it usually takes about two years to become emotionally stable after the death of a spouse. The surviving spouse begins to wonder at times whether life will ever be fulfilling and happy again. A woman whose husband died said that, even months later, when something significant would happen, she would say, "You know, I have got to tell Gerald about that tonight whenever he gets home." And then she would remember: Gerald is not coming home tonight—or ever. She said a year, two years, after his death, she would be sitting in church and not even be thinking about him, but she would see the back of a man's head that reminded her of her husband, or there would be a hymn sung that she could remember his singing, and suddenly the tears would just flow again. The memories and emotions would stay with her that long! So it may well be that you or someone close to you can identify with the grief process that Naomi was going through.

The second category of singles that we minister to are those who have gone through the pain of divorce. A friend of mine from Bible college went through a bitter divorce some time ago.

He was a respected minister, but his wife just ran off with another man. He was devastated by that. He didn't expect it. He talked with me about what a traumatic experience it is to go through a divorce. He said, "Bob, in many ways, I think it's more difficult to go through a divorce than it is to go through the death of your spouse." When somebody dies, you usually don't blame yourself. But in a divorce there is constant guilt. When somebody dies, you say good-bye and you know that it is over, as hard as that is. But in divorce you keep seeing the person and reliving the death of your feelings. When a mate dies, you have the positive memory of their love, but in divorce you have to live with the reality of rejection and failure. When a mate dies, you receive comfort from friends. But when there is divorce, your friends don't know what to say. Sometimes they ignore you; sometimes they become your enemies because they side with your spouse.

If you have experienced the pain of divorce, you can understand some of the feelings that Ruth, this young widow, was going through since her husband had died.

A third category of single people we minister to are those who have never married. Since 1970, the proportion of persons aged 25 to 29 who have never married has more than doubled for men and has tripled for women. Some have never married because they have been disillusioned by people whom they have dated. Some have never married because they are disillusioned by the example that their parents set. Some have not married because the right person has not come along, and they are waiting, trying to be wise in selection. Some of them are very frustrated with that. They say, "I am trying to live in God's will, trying to do what is right, but the right person hasn't come along. Where is God?" Some have not married because they would rather be happy single than married and not happy.

Wherever you are in the single life, there is always somebody trying to fix you up, always somebody trying to match you with somebody. When my son was twenty-four years old and not married, my wife was really concerned about him. He was living miles away from home, living alone, and almost every time he called, she was asking him about his date life—and she wasn't very subtle about it. She was encouraging him; she was just concerned that he needed somebody to be his companion.

When he brought home a girlfriend, my home became hectic all weekend before they arrived! My wife was getting the house clean and planning the meals. She wanted me to mow the grass that I had just mowed two days before, but it had to look right. Every minor detail was crucial!

My son said, "Dad, now, I really like this girl, and she is really a good Christian girl. Her dad is a principal of a Christian school, and she sings and plays the piano in her church. She is not perfect—she is a Baptist—but we will try to see what we can do to convert her." He said, "Dad, she is really pretty, too. She is serving as Miss Augusta. But," he said, "she sang the National Anthem at a Hawks game in Atlanta at the Omni, and the P.A. announcer made a mistake and introduced her as Miss August." He said, "There were cat calls and whistles—and she was devastated." He said, "Dad, if you hear rumors that I am dating a *Playboy* Centerfold, that is not true. She is Miss Augusta."

If you are single, you know there is always somebody, parents included, trying to encourage you along. The story of Naomi and Ruth is a pertinent story, but it's also a positive one. It starts out with sadness because the mates have died, but it winds up in a positive way with fulfillment.

From Sadness to Joy

In her loneliness, Naomi decided that she was going to move back to Judah, and both her daughters-in-law were so fond of her that they decided that they would go along. They started out together, but then Naomi changed her mind.

> Then Naomi said to her two daughters-in-law, "Go back, each of you, to your mother's home. May the Lord show kindness to you, as you have shown to your dead and to me. May the Lord grant that each of you will find rest in the home of another husband" (Ruth 1:8, 9)

Naomi was concerned that her daughters-in-law be remarried. She went on to say, in essence, "Look, your chances of getting married again are not as good if you come back with me to Judah as if you stay here in your homeland. I am not going to have more sons. You are better off if you stay here." So Orpah, one of her daughters-in-law, went back home. But Ruth insisted on going along with Naomi.

Now, look at verses 16 and 17. Here is a passage of Scripture that you often hear read at weddings, and I think it's a good statement for husbands and wives to make to one another. Initially, however, this statement was made by Ruth to her mother-in-law:

> Don't urge me to leave you or to turn back from you. Where you go I will go, and where you stay I will stay. Your people will be my people, and your God my God. Where you die I will die, and there I will be buried. May the Lord deal with me, be it ever so severely, if anything but death separates you and me.

So Ruth went on with Naomi to a new land. That tells us that Ruth not only loved Naomi, but she was a very adventuresome single woman. She didn't lock herself in the room and wallow in self-pity. She began to search for a new life-style even though that was risky. She was not pursuing a new life-style to get a better husband; she just wanted a different life, and she was concerned about Naomi. That is one of the things that made her attractive. That sense of security and independence made people respect her.

Generally speaking, it seems the more aggressive a person is and the more anxious he is to get married, the more he turns people off! Have you noticed that? I remember in college, guys would say, "Boy, don't date her. She is after her M-R-S degree!" What did they mean? They meant there was something wrong—she was too anxious to get married, and that made her less attractive somehow. Ruth was an attractive person because she was not obsessed with the idea of getting married again.

In chapter 2 of the book of Ruth, one reads that their initial experience in Bethlehem was that Ruth went to work. Verse 2: "Ruth . . . said to Naomi, 'Let me go to the fields and pick up the leftover grain behind anyone in whose eyes I find favor.'" Don't miss the significance of that: Ruth was an alien, a young woman, alone. She was very vulnerable in the harvest fields. But she was determined to provide for herself and for her mother-in-law.

To pick up leftover grain in the harvest field was not a very glamorous or lucrative job. In Leviticus 19, God instructed landowners to leave what the harvesters had missed so that the poor, the alien, the widow, and the fatherless could glean for their needs. Gleaning in the fields was much like going out and walking the expressway and picking up aluminum cans for an occupation today. But Ruth went to work, and we respect her for that.

While she was working in the fields, Ruth was noticed by the owner of the field, a man named Boaz. The Bible doesn't say that Ruth made a big play for him. He just noticed her.

> Boaz asked the foreman of his harvesters, "Whose young woman is that?"
>
> The foreman replied, "She is the Moabitess who came back from Moab with Naomi. . . . She went into the field and has worked steadily from morning till now, except for a short rest in the shelter" (Ruth 2:5-7).

If you are walking in God's will, He will see to it that the right person comes along in His time. But it is essential that you walk in God's will. If Ruth had been out to a night club or singles' bar, I doubt she would have met Boaz. She did what was right, and God brought her into contact with this wealthy landowner.

Boaz introduced himself, and they struck up a pleasant conversation. Boaz granted Ruth special favors. He asked her how she was doing and gave her hints on how to increase the harvest and where to go for a free drink of water. Overwhelmed with gratitude, Ruth asked him, "Why are you being so kind to me, a foreigner?"

"I have heard about how kind you have been to Naomi," he replied, "and she is a relative of mine. I respect you for that."

At mealtime, and Boaz said to her, "Come over here and eat with me." The plot thickens! This gets very romantic, too. After lunch, as she got up to go back to glean, Boaz gave orders to his men, "Even if she gathers among the sheaves, don't embarrass her. Rather, pull out some stalks for her from the bundles and leave them for her to pick up, and don't rebuke her" (verses 15 and 16).

When Ruth got home that night, she had a large sack of grain. Naomi was impressed. "What has happened?" she asked. Ruth then explained how Boaz had helped out.

Naomi replied, "The Lord bless him. He has not stopped showing kindness to us." Then she added, "This man is a close relative—and he is a bachelor, and he is rich." Well, the Bible didn't say that last part, but you know she must have said that!

Ruth said, "Well, he has invited me to stay in his field until the harvesters are finished."

And Naomi said, "That is good; you will be safer there."

In chapter 3, Naomi really began to play Cupid. Verse 1: "My daughter, should I not try to find a home for you, where you will be well provided for? Is not Boaz, with whose servant girls you have been, a kinsman of ours? Tonight he will be winnowing barley on the threshing floor. . . ." There was a custom in that day for the owners to sleep with their grain whenever it was harvested so that they could protect it. Naomi was saying, "I know where Boaz will be tonight, so here is what I want you to do. You wash, you perfume yourself, you put on your best clothes, and you look nice. And then you go to the barn where he is working, and after he eats and lies down to sleep, you go lie down at his feet, and he will tell you what to do."

What is going on here?

Well, actually this is not immoral; it's a proposal. Ruth was instructed to prepare herself like a bride and announce to Boaz that she was interested and available. Listen to what happened, beginning with verse 8 in chapter 3. I like the wording of *The Living Bible* here; it makes it clearer.

Suddenly, around midnight, he wakened and sat up, startled. There was a woman lying at his feet!

"Who are you?" he demanded.

"It's I, sir—Ruth," she replied. "Make me your wife according to God's law. For you are my close relative."

"Thank God for a girl like you!" he exclaimed. [I guess so!] "For you are being even kinder to Naomi now than before. Naturally, you'd prefer a younger man, even though poor. [He kind of works in that "poor" angle a little.] But you have put aside your personal desires [so that you can give Naomi an heir by marrying me]. Now, don't worry about a thing, my child; I'll handle all the details, for everyone knows what a wonderful person you are" (Ruth 3:8-11, TLB).

Verse 11 is translated in the New International Version like this: "All my fellow townsmen know that you are a woman of noble character."

In the final chapter, Ruth and Boaz are married. There are a few legal problems that have to be worked out, but it has a happy ending for both of them. Verse 13 of chapter 4 reads, "So Boaz took Ruth and she became his wife. Then he went to her. . . ." Notice that there was no physical relationship until after they were married. And the Lord enabled her to conceive, and she gave birth to a son.

Guidelines for Single People

This is such a practical story for single people. There are several pragmatic guidelines we can glean from it. Number one, if you have experienced the loss of a mate, *understand that grief is a long process*. Be patient. If people say it takes two years before your emotions settle down to become stable following the death of a mate, and if divorce is very similar to that, you need to be very patient. Since that is such a stressful time, why not use that time to draw closer to the Lord instead of dating here and there.

I once asked several people who had experienced divorce to meet with me to help me understand the dynamics affecting divorced people. Two women, who had gone through a divorce over six years before, both said the same thing. They said it was horrible the first year. But as bad as it was, that was a time when they grew more in their Christian lives than they ever had before. They said, "I prayed more and the Scriptures comforted me and came alive for me." One of them remarried after six years, and the other had not yet remarried. But they both confirmed that they were not anywhere near ready that first year to jump into another relationship, even though they felt they had a Scriptural right to do so.

A man in that meeting said, when he went through his divorce, he was determined to remain faithful to Christ. He said, "I chose therefore not to date at all the whole first year, because I knew I was so emotionally unstable I would be vulnerable to the wrong kind of relationship." It takes a long time to settle emotions down. Dating and remarriage don't cure it; so be patient.

The second principle is this: *learn to be content single.* Accept the fact that singleness may be God's will for your life. I know some single people who have made themselves miserable because they are convinced that, if they are not married, they can't be fulfilled as a person. I know married people who make themselves miserable because they think they are not happy because they are not single. I heard of a man and his wife who were celebrating their twenty-fifth wedding anniversary, and he broke down in tears. She said, "What is wrong with you? Why are you so emotional?"

He said, "I just remembered, on our honeymoon when I said I was so mad at you, I could kill you. And you said that if I killed you, I would go to jail for at least twenty-five years."

She said, "Oh, honey, don't worry about that. I have not held that against you. I forgave you for that a long time ago."

He said, "I know, but I was just thinking: if I had done it, today I would be a free man."

When you talk to some married people, they say, "Boy, I wish I were single." Many single people look at the other side of the fence and say, "Oh, if only I were married." Some singles are programmed to believe that the only way that they can be fulfilled is to have a marriage relationship. If marriage doesn't come their way, they feel inferior or rejected, and some desperately jump into a wrong relationship.

You must understand that the single life *can be* God's will for you, and it can be a very *fulfilling* life. Some of you who are single right now have better communication and closer companionship with friends than many married people have with their mates. Our society has so exaggerated the importance of sexual fulfillment in life that some people have the impression that one cannot be a whole person if he can't have his physical passion satisfied. That is not true. Jesus Christ, the greatest man who ever lived, was single. And Paul said, "I have learned the secret of being content in any and every situation. . . . I can do everything through [Christ] who gives me strength" (Philippians 4:12, 13).

God has not put the key to your happiness in the pocket of somebody that you have never met. It's in your own attitude. Make up your mind that you are going to be happy single, and if the right person comes along, fine; and if not, you are going to be as contented as you can possibly be.

Our church has a women's retreat each spring—they call it "Spring Fling." This past year, Lucy Swindoll was their featured speaker. I heard a number of great comments about her speeches. She is single, in her fifties, a great author, and a vibrant personality. She said that her favorite verse of Scripture is, "If any man would come after me, let him!" She said, "I'm not chasing anybody down, but I'm not going to prohibit them either." You can be happy single.

Third—and this is very, very important—*maintain your character regardless.* Boaz had no relations with Ruth until after they were married. "Everybody knows what a noble character you are," he told Ruth. Now, when you are alone, you are vulnerable. You want somebody to comfort you and hold you. It may surprise you, even though you are a Christian with strong convictions how quickly you can fall into a physical relationship if you do not decide in advance what your standards are going to be.

I hear all kinds of rationalizations for singles. They will say, "Oh, you don't understand. The temptations today are so great." "God's grace will forgive me." "We are going to get married anyway." "You can't be expected to control your passions when you are thirty-five or forty years old." Some are using sex to hang onto a shaky relationship, concluding that it's better to live in sin than it is to be lonely.

I know it's very difficult in this era to maintain purity when you are not married. It is difficult, but it's not impossible. I know people who do it. Joseph was nearly thirty, alone in a foreign country, and virile when he was approached by Potiphar's wife. She tried to seduce him, but Joseph said, "I can't do this thing and sin against my God."

If you think it's too difficult and you think it's impossible, would you remember something? It wasn't exactly easy for Jesus to go to the cross and die for you, either. He said, "If you are not willing to deny yourself and take up your cross and follow after me, you are not worthy of being my disciple" (cf. Matthew 10:37, 38). And you have no right to ask God to bless your future if you are flagrantly and continuously defying His command to flee fornication. I just can't make it any simpler than that. Guard your character, and trust that in the end God will bless.

Fourth, *be very cautious about remarriage*. The number of remarriages in this country has increased by sixty-three percent since 1970. But if you are a Christian, would you read the Scripture very carefully and determine whether or not you have God's permission to remarry. First Corinthians 7:39 states you have permission to remarry if your mate has died. As I understand Matthew 19:9 and 1 Corinthians 7:15, the Bible indicates that God permits divorce and remarriage in the case of unfaithfulness or abandonment. But we need also to consider 1 Corinthians 7:10:

> To the married I give this command. . . . A wife must not separate from her husband. But if she does, she must remain unmarried or else be reconciled to her husband. And a husband must not divorce his wife.

I know of a woman whose husband became an alcoholic, his personality changed, he began to abuse her, he began to abuse the children, and she said, "It's God's will for me to get a divorce and get out of this marriage for my own protection and for the protection of my children." I would agree. "But," she added, "I don't believe it's God's will for me to remarry. I am just going to pray for him that he would repent and turn to Christ and we can be reconciled."

Study those passages, and then respond with a submissive spirit to God's will. Any time you get into a situation where you say, "I know this isn't what the Bible says, but I think this is going to make me happier," you are on dangerous ground because you are thinking that you know more about what is going to make you happy in the future than God does. He knows all things. God isn't out to hurt you. He wants to protect you from that which could devastate you. And even if you have Scriptural permission to remarry, be very cautious in entering a new relationship. According to the *U.S. News and World Report*, there is a sixty percent divorce rate for remarriages. Remarried couples face from three to ten times the stress as those in first marriages. That includes financial problems, relocation, the tension of step parenting, dealing with former spouses, and more. So be open to the idea of remarriage, if you think it's God's will, but don't aggressively pursue it. If it's God's will, He will make it happen.

The most important criterion to any relationship is that the person you marry be a Christian and have Christ at the center of his life. Second Corinthians 6:14 says, "Do not be yoked together with unbelievers. For what do righteousness and wickedness have in common?" It cannot be God's will for you to marry somebody who doesn't share your convictions about Christ. In light of that truth, "What in the world would you be doing running around at singles bars? Can it really be that you are going to find somebody there who is going to share your convictions about Christ?"

One couple—both partners had been victims of unfaithfulness in previous marriages—met at our church. Mike came to know Gwenn in one of the singles classes here, attending social functions together for a long period of time. Then eventually, after they became friends, he asked her out. For four months, he didn't even kiss her. He kissed her several times on the forehead, and she wondered, "What in the world is wrong with this guy?" But he admitted, "I was afraid that if I even kissed her, I wouldn't be able to control my passions, and I was determined that I was going to be a Christian." After they determined that it was God's will for them to get married, they were married in less than two months. Put yourself in a situation where you are meeting other Christians, and make sure you are controlling your passions, so that you marry in God's will.

The final principle that we need to learn from this story is, if you decide to remarry, *give yourself to that marriage wholeheartedly*. Ruth gave herself to Boaz completely. If you have been hurt in a relationship, there is a real tendency to protect yourself in the next one. You become paranoid, and you hear about people having pre-nuptial agreements with all kind of contingencies, and you wonder if you shouldn't do something like that. If the marriage is God's will, it should be regarded as sacred and permanent—with no strings attached. You are instructed to give yourself completely to the other in marriage; the two become one. The marriage has to take precedence over every other relationship—your spouse over every other friend or family member. If you are not willing to make that kind of commitment, if you are not willing to take that kind of risk, then you are not ready to get married. Without such commitment, your marriage will have little chance of survival. When you get into that new relationship, give yourself wholeheartedly, as unto the Lord.

Before I close, I must say a word to a significant group of people that I have not addressed in this entire book. There may be a number of people reading this book who have been divorced and remarried already, and when the subject of divorce is discussed, it probably creates questions in their minds:

"Should I have worked at my first marriage harder?"

"Was I outside God's will when I remarried?"

"Am I living in adultery?"

"Am I welcome in the church?"

"If I did God's will right now, would I divorce my present mate and go back to my first one and try to restore that relationship?"

The answer to that last question is no. According to Deuteronomy 24, you're not to return to the original relationship.

God's grace is a marvelous thing. I say this with fear and trembling because that grace is not something to be taken lightly. But when we come to Him in submission and true repentance, He can wipe the slate clean—no matter how black it's been. He can help us to start over. I say this with fear and trembling because in no way do I want to leave the impression with others that they can presume on God's grace in advance. But God can forgive, and God can bless a relationship that really shouldn't have started in the first place. There could be no more sordid story than that of David and Bathsheba. They had no right to be together. And there were horrible consequences that came to that relationship. But David pleaded for God's forgiveness. God washed him whiter than snow, and though the first child born to David and Bathsheba died, eventually Solomon was born to David and Bathsheba, a son who knew the Lord and led the nation of Israel.

You can't go back and unscramble eggs, and you can't go back and undo mistakes of the past. Trying to do that generally just compounds the problem. But you can pick up where you are right now and say, "Lord, there are so many complicated situations, but I ask Your forgiveness of my sin. I thank You for Your grace. I pledge to You that I will walk in Your will from this day forward."

The woman at the well had been divorced five times, and she was living with a man to whom she was not married, but Jesus didn't reject her. He invited her into His kingdom. He welcomed her. He took advantage of her evangelistic efforts, and He gave her renewal (John 4).

My mother married my father before my father became a Christian. That might not have been in the perfect will of God. But God has blessed. I am convinced of that. Second Corinthians 5:17 says, "If any man be in Christ, he is a new creature: old things are passed away; behold, all things are become new" (KJV). The important matter is to walk in God's will from this day forward.

The main characters in this study all started over, each finding fulfillment in obedience. Boaz, who had been single most of his life, married a wonderful wife. Ruth was given a godly husband, and her life was blessed with a baby boy she named Obed. And Naomi remained single, but she experienced joy and fulfillment, too.

Before you close this book, would you read two verses from the end of the book of Ruth? Ruth brings her little baby and puts him into the lap of the grandmother-in-law, and we read,

Then Naomi took the child, laid him in her lap and cared for him. The women living there said, "Naomi has a son." And they named him Obed. He was the father of Jesse, the father of David (Ruth 4:16, 17).

Through this line came Jesus, who was to be the Savior of the world. "God works in mysterious ways, His wonders to perform." He can help us start over and experience joy if we will patiently walk in His will and allow His Word to guide our lives and our marriages.